PEOPLE AT WAR

1914-1918

in preparation

People at War 1939-1945

PEOPLE AT WAR

1914-1918

Edited by

Michael Moynihan

DAVID & CHARLES: NEWTON ABBOT

940.315 MOYN

79643

0 7153 6273 9

Set in 11 on 13pt. Baskerville
and Printed in Great Britain
by John Sherratt & Son Limited
for David & Charles (Holdings) Limited
South Devon House Newton Abbot Devon.

Contents

FOREWORD

Foreword

The idea for this book (and an ensuing volume covering World War II) followed an article in *The Sunday Times* which quoted from some of the latest 'finds' of the Imperial War Museum and invited readers to send in their own war stories. The response was overwhelming, ranging from faded pocket-diaries and letters to bulky journals written in retrospect. It is from the best of these, and from the best of the Imperial War Museum's recent acquisitions, that *People at War* has been compiled.

A reawakening of interest in the two world wars (mirrored most obviously in a spate of television series and the mass book-stall sales of illustrated war histories) derives from a variety of reasons: a growing nostalgia for the days when Britain was still Great, a bastion of freedom against the tides of aggression; a backward look, from an age when we are all at the mercy of a mere finger on the button, to the last great wars to be fought 'conventionally' by opposing armies, navies and air forces; a personal reidentification with times when life seemed heightened by danger and conflict; a reassuring reminder that today's violence is minimal compared with then.

But to many, the absorbing interest must lie in the reaction of the individual to dangers and privations that tax him to the limit. It has been a revealing as well as moving experience to follow the day-by-day diary entries of that young Guards officer, Lt William St Leger, from boyish enthusiasm to anguish over his fallen comrades, knowing that his own half wished for death in action lies at the end. It has been revealing and moving in a different way to read of the ordeals of three Tommies, rarely depicted until now, in journals written in recent retirement by men we too readily categorise in such vague and comfortable phrases as 'war veterans', unaware of the obsessive memories that still haunt them.

A vast amount has been written about the Great War (as it is still significantly known), much of it in the form of scholarly reconstructions of its major battles, concerned with strategy and tactics, the bunglings of generals and the efficacy of new weapons. In the accounts that follow, edited to indicate the man inside the uniform as much as for their dramatic content, there is little of import for the historian. But for the general reader here is eloquent testimony to the enduring qualities of man, qualities that were never more tested than in the midst of this carnage, this seemingly futile waste.

Any attempt by later generations to understand the role of the civilian soldier in the trenches must to some extent be subjective. To those born in the last three decades, even such motivating forces as patriotism, sense of duty, discipline, *esprit de corps*, must seem strangely unreal, even naïve. To my own generation, brought up between the wars, the Great War was more than past history, dead and done with. We felt it there behind us, casting an ominous shadow out towards the war we dimly knew must lie ahead.

In the minor public school I attended, 'Lest We Forget' had a dual interpretation. Jingoism still prevailed, in the school chaplain's homilies, on the OTC parade ground, marching on church parade through the streets of the town to the sound of bugle and drum and the sergeant-major's growl, 'Put some *swank* into it!' At summer camp near Aldershot, khaki-clad contingents from public schools throughout the country, swaggering and sweating, stalking each other in mock battles,

kept the flag flying. War was equated with the sonnets of
Rupert Brooke, with the stained glass piety of Armistice Day—
the two minutes' silence, 'We shall remember them', and Last
Post.

Opposing this was a growing wave of revulsion against war
as it had now been revealed, under all those trappings, in a
spate of books that began to pour out ten years after the war's
ending in all the major combatant countries, like a spontaneous
bursting of floodgates on a truth too long repressed. Most
notable were the memoirs of Robert Graves, Siegfried Sassoon,
Edmund Blunden, Remarque's *All Quiet on the Western Front*,
Hemingway's *A Farewell to Arms*, Richard Aldington's *Death of
a Hero*. And there were the war poets. For some of us, still half-
enamoured of the bitter-sweet cadences of Rupert Brooke, a
first reading of Wilfred Owen had a traumatic effect:

What passing-bells for these who die as cattle?
  Only the monstrous anger of the guns.
  Only the stuttering rifles' rapid rattle
Can patter out their hasty orisons . . .

Many people's conception of trench warfare must be
coloured by the heightened perceptions of the soldier-poets.
But a wider reading makes it clear that the suffering and the
slaughter, the 'pity of war', was by no means the whole story.
Charles Carrington, whose *A Subaltern's War*, published in
1929, was something of a counterblast to the prevailing
pacifism, has even suggested that a largely erroneous picture
of the front-line soldier has come to be accepted. In one of the
essays contributed by eminent World War I veterans to
Promise of Greatness, a memorial volume for the fiftieth anniversary of the Armistice, he writes: 'I never meet an "old
sweat", as we liked to describe ourselves, who accepts or enjoys
the figure in which we are now presented. Just smile and make
an old soldier's wry joke when you see yourself on the television

screen, agonised and woebegone, trudging from disaster to disaster, knee-deep in moral as well as physical mud, hesitant about your purpose, submissive to a harsh irrelevant discipline, mistrustful of your commanders . . .'

In some respects at least, the three former Tommies, from whose journals extracts are given here, would seem to be nearer that popular conception than Carrington allows, particularly in their resentment at having to put up with point-less regulations and arbitrary discipline, their mistrust of most commanders not close to them, and the lack of purpose they felt in much of what they had to undergo. But certainly there is evidence enough that life could acquire a richer savour when death lay so close at hand.

'I was always happier up the line,' writes former Rifleman Tommy Atkins, though admitting that 'we lived like rats, fed like rats and died like rats', and that, in his journal, he has 'played down the horrors'. And Lt St Leger, who can be seen as epitomising the public school patriot who unquestioningly swopped cricket bat for rifle, as though war was but a more challenging, more rewarding game, only rarely hints at a torment of spirit implicit in the nightmares he relates. The horrors he seems to take in his stride, and some of his descrip-tions of battles have an almost exuberant ring about them:

> . . . We fixed bayonets. We passed a trench just this side of the brow of the hill held by a machine-gun company of a line regiment. Our men joked and laughed with them as they passed. Several hares got up and ran about everywhere to the men's huge delight. I saw Gillie lighting his pipe. There were a lot of cavalry following up on our right some distance behind. We went over the hill deploying into line at the top, under fire the whole time . . .

To make sense of much that happened on the Western Front it is necessary to be aware of the social and emotional climate of the times. When war broke out, England (as Great Britain was then commonly known) was the envy of the world, hub of the greatest empire in history, and its social structure seemed to most to be too firmly rooted to be seriously threatened by rebellious spirits like the Suffragettes or the trade unions. A privileged upper class, an industrious middle class, an under-privileged but mostly subservient working class, entered on the war each knowing its proper station in life (it went without saying that an officer was a product of the public schools).

The country had been virtually at peace for the past hundred years. The recent Boer War had been an exciting but remote affair, rather in the nature of an away match between the 'soldiers of the King' and an inferior breed. And it was in much the same spirit, 'for England's glorious name', that the first troops sailed for France and the first volunteers, of all classes, rallied to their country's call. The war would be over by Christmas: God *would* make us mightier yet. Only the more perceptive were aware that an era was coming to an end.

'Buttons, badges and boots highly polished, we swaggered down the hill, everyone in perfect step,' writes Bert Chaney, describing his arrival in France early in 1915 in his journal 'A Lad Goes to War'. 'We'd show these Frenchmen what a London Terrier Regiment was like. Now we had arrived in France the war was as good as over, so we thought.' It was a mood quite unlike that at the start of World War II, which had been seen a long time coming, where the enemy was a known quantity and one could only grit one's teeth and get on with it, civilian and conscript alike. What comes out strongly from most World War I accounts from the trenches is an absence of hostility towards the enemy, coupled with a growing gulf between front line and home front.

'We looked at them as "old Jerry" across No Man's Land, to be bashed when we had the chance,' writes Atkins. 'No real hatred, not even when we were being heavily shelled. It was "I wonder what's upset Jerry tonight?"' In many ways, indeed, there was a closer affinity with 'Jerry' or 'Fritz', sharing the same rigours and dangers (mud, freezing cold, hunger, rats, lice, as much as shells, bullets, poison gas) than with people back home, lapping up stories of Hun atrocities and the jingoistic sentimentality of the music hall.

In the last chapter of this book, the diary extracts of Ernest Cooper, redoubtable town clerk of the 'little Frontier Coast Town of Southwold', are indicative of the civilian attitude to the war. The fuss made of zeppelin raids (so puny compared with the World War II blitzes), of occasional coastal bombardments, of billeting, rationing, scarcities, seems out of all proportion to what was being endured on the Western Front. At Southwold, on 31 July 1917, they could hear clearly the distant rumble of the guns as the British launched their doomed offensive over the cloying mud of the Ypres salient. Cooper merely notes in his diary that the barrage 'produced as usual a torrential fall of rain'. An industrious, self-sacrificing patriot, mainstay of the local war effort, he scarcely alludes in his journal to all that was going on out there. It could have been another war, another world.

For those who knew it intimately, it could be a world one longed to get out of, then hankered to get back to. 'Personally I am sick of it and want to get away back to the front', writes Lt William Read, a pioneer pilot with the Royal Flying Corps, on leave in a Paris where 'the women will not let us alone', and he feels 'such a chocolate soldier walking about in uniform with everybody staring at me'.

What drew men back, and what held them there, was a feeling that lies at the heart of most of these diaries and memoirs, a feeling inadequately expressed as *camaraderie* or *esprit de corps*. To the front line soldier existence became bearable because shared, not anonymously but within the familiar confines of a section, a platoon. And it was in that process of sharing, when a man was judged by more than rank or class or accent, that he could scale heights as well as plumb depths.

When R. C. Sherriff's *Journey's End* was first staged professionally in 1929, a critic detected 'an underlying poetic feeling, not a poetry of the imagination so much, but rather a poetry of human concern'. It was a feeling that still came powerfully across when a West End revival of the play, in 1972, drew unexpectedly large and diversified audiences. To many, watching the comings and goings in that dug-out as the shells whined and detonated in the nightmare world outside, the stilted dialogue and long-outdated slang, the public school ethics and stiff upper lip reactions, must have seemed at first almost ludicrously unreal. But no one laughed. We sat gripped, and moved. And when the final life-obliterating crunch came and the curtain fell, it was that 'poetry of human concern' that lingered in the mind, and the question 'Did they die in vain?' seemed somehow irrelevant.

It is such a poetry, less consciously contrived, that underlies and links the diaries and journals from which this book has been compiled, and which lift them above mere records of a war that has passed into history, dead and done with.

Michael Moynihan

AIR AND LAND

1 Cavalryman in the Flying Machines

On 12 August 1914, eight days after the outbreak of war, Lt W. R. Read, a pilot with the Royal Flying Corps recently seconded from the King's Dragoon Guards, was sent by his commanding officer into Lympne, near Hythe on the Kentish coast, to purchase as many motor-car inner tubes as he could lay his hands on. They were distributed among the pilots waiting to take off from the nearby aerodrome—lightweight lifebelts in the event of forced landings in the Channel on the way to the war in France.

With its primitive, flimsy machines, the RFC, formed only two years before and numbering 105 officers, 755 men and 63 aeroplanes, was regarded as something of a joke by the British Expeditionary Force when it made its début in the skies over France and Belgium a week later. But within days it became apparent that information about troop movements obtained by aerial reconnaissance could be of vital importance. Without it the retreat from Mons would have been even more of a massacre. And soon artillery officers were relying on these daring young men in their flying machines to range their batteries on to enemy targets. A new dimension had been added to warfare.

The day-by-day diary kept by Read during these critical weeks and throughout the rest of the war is of historic as well as human interest. It records the teething troubles of the RFC, when pilots were as much at the mercy of the elements and the

inadequacies of their 'stick-and-string' machines as of enemy gunfire. And it traces its gradual growth into a lethal striking force, forerunner of the aerial armadas of World War II, beginning to strike terror into the hearts of the civilian population in Germany.

At the end of the war the Royal Air Force numbered 291,175 officers and men and 22,171 machines. Read himself—now a major in command of a bomber squadron, decorated with the AFC, DFC and MC—was only stopped by the Armistice from leading a 'hush-hush' expedition to Czechoslovakia, from which to launch the first, morale-shattering raids on Berlin.

The eight hastily scrawled volumes of Read's wartime diary reveal him as very much the man of action, and give little hint as to his emotional make-up. But an unfinished autobiography he wrote after his retirement from the RAF at the end of the last war is revealing. Born in 1886, son of a wealthy businessman, he had an unhappy childhood. He was afraid of his father, who used to line up his children 'like soldiers' in the day nursery of their Hampstead home if any of them had done wrong, and whom he never remembers laughing.

'I always seemed to be in some sort of trouble as a child, breaking things or upsetting them,' he recalls. 'I had an inquisitive turn of mind, with a mixture of destructiveness in it. I remember incurring everyone's wrath one day when I guillotined several dolls by steamrollering their necks under the rocking horse.'

He could not remember any occasion when his mother showed any affection for him—possibly, he suggests, because she was preoccupied with regular additions to the family. She died when he was ten, and his father, broken-hearted, died a year later. Unhappy at King Edward VI's Grammar School, Southampton, he left at the age of fourteen to take private tuition. A concentrated spell of cramming scraped him into Cambridge in 1905, where he blossomed out. He had already

decided to join the Army and devoted a good deal of his energies to sport—rowing, soccer, boxing, fencing.

In retrospect Read is grateful to 'Pa'. 'Though I hated every moment with him, he used to nag and bully me so, the results of his hard work have meant that for all the adult years of my life, war apart, I have been able to go my own way, indulge in my own pursuits and live independently. He endowed me with a happy, carefree future life.'

In 1907 he joined the King's Dragoon Guards and felt immediately at home in a self-contained world of traditional etiquette and boisterous camaraderie, where horsemanship and sportsmanship counted for most. Because of his prowess at fisticuffs, he was nicknamed 'Jimmy' after Jim Corbett, then champion professional boxer. And he describes as the six happiest years of his life those he spent with the regiment at Umballa in the Punjab, a good deal of it on leave shooting in Kashmir. It was regarded as part of a cavalryman's education, he explains, to go on such adventurous trips with a native bearer, teaching self-reliance, resourcefulness and an eye for country.

In 1912 he was granted a year's leave to go shooting through the wilds of Central Asia. Awarded the title 'Best shot of the Regiment' the year before, he achieved an impressive bag, including a Mongolian tiger and a snow leopard. And the hazards he phlegmatically encountered with his faithful bearer during a trek in which his mode of transport ranged from pony, mule, yak, camel, and Chinese cart to the sleigh in which he ended up at a remote station on the Trans-Siberian Railway, might partly explain his seeming fearlessness in the cockpit of a biplane over the Western Front.

It was at the end of this leave in England, that he took a pilot's course and got 'bitten with flying'. In December 1913 he was seconded to the RFC. Training involved what he describes as a 'fair amount of crashery'. Time off he mostly spent with his closest friend, Lt Shekleton (frequently mentioned in the early part of the diaries), trout-fishing in the Avon, speeding around the countryside in his new Mercedes-Benz.

Then, in June 1914, they learned that the RFC would, after all, play an active role in the pending war. 'There was feverish excitement, everyone taking a great new interest in their machine. I had been issued with my own Henri Farman biplane and got busy in the workshops making spare parts. Captain Herbert, our Flight Commander, saw me one day making a bullet-proof seat to sit on. "Good lor," he said, "your machine will never get off the ground with all those things." I was glad I carried on. Later that seat stopped me from a nasty wound.'

On 13 August, four days after the BEF under Field-Marshal Sir John French had landed in France to challenge the German advance through Belgium, three squadrons of the RFC took off from Dover for Amiens. Read's engine was 'not running well' and he took 2 hours 50 minutes to fly the 120 miles, to find 49 aircraft parked on the aviation ground. Three days later they flew to Mauberge, showered with flowers wherever they landed en route. They were 40 miles from the Germans. But already, Read records, there had been nineteen accidents, some fatal, since take-off in England. 'If we have all these accidents now, whatever will it be like when we go into action,' he wonders, and grimly adds: 'However, the estimate is that no more than 5 per cent of us who have come out with the Corps will go back, so cheerio!'

During the retreat to the Marne in the next two weeks, the RFC, one jump ahead of the Germans as they kept up their vital reconnaissance, set up fleeting headquarters in nine different localities, and Read's daily entries are understandably unelaborated. Something of what may be missing is indicated by the description in his autobiographical jottings of one of his first reconnaissance flights. It refers to Captain Jackson, his observer until the end of the retreat, 'a very cheery bird, always thirsting for blood'. Read describes him as the best observer with the RFC and claims that orders for the retreat were based considerably on his reports, which revealed not only the enemy's progress but the fact that the French army was falling back fast on the right.

'One day, after our reconnaissance over Mons and Charleroi, Jackson spotted a German Taube machine. I had also seen him but we had done our job and I did not want a fight. Jackson was always bloodthirsty, however, and the following shouted conversation ensued:

'Jackson: "Look, old boy!"

'Me: "Yes, I know."

'Jackson: "I think we ought to go for him, old boy."

'Me: "Better get home with your report."

'Jackson: "I think we ought to go for him, old boy."

'Me: "All right."

'I changed course for him and, as we passed the Taube, Jackson got in two shots with the rifle. We turned and passed each other again with no obvious result. This happened three or four times. Then, "Have you got a revolver, old boy? My ammunition's all gone." I, feeling rather sick of the proceedings, said "Yes. But no ammo." "Give it me, old boy, and this time fly past him as close as you can." I carried out instructions and, to my amazement, as soon as we got opposite the Taube, Jackson, with my Army issue revolver grasped by the barrel, threw it at the Taube's propeller. Of course it missed and then, honour satisfied, we turned for home.'

The diary starts, at Mauberge, on 22 August when Sir John French, with two British divisions, was marching to confront two German army corps in the bloody battle of Mons before the retreat forced upon him by his precarious position. Omitted from these extracts are certain details Read invariably recorded —time of Reveille (usually around 6 am at this period), weather conditions, prevailing winds—and routine or repetitive items.

'*22 August.* Today the French distinguished themselves by bringing down one of their own airships. They also often fire at us and there is quite as much to fear from one's own side as from the Germans as one leaves the ground. Two machines that went out this morning on reconnaissance came back with several bullet holes in them. In one the observer was shot in the stomach. Herbert, Shekleton, Fuller and I are the 4 pilots in our Flight. We do more flying than most other flights probably because Henri is a more reliable machine and is always ready. Shek. came back last night with six shot holes in his planes. One bullet missed the petrol tank only by an inch.

'*23 August*. Last night 1st, 2nd and 3rd Infantry Brigades passed through Mauberge. They marched all night, making for Mons. This morning we can hear guns firing from the direction of Charleroi. Yesterday afternoon Waterfall and Bayly went off to reconnoitre on an Avro. They have not come back yet.' [The RFC's first casualties from enemy action, they were shot down by rifle fire and both killed.—*MM*.] 'Yesterday morning a German aeroplane passed over here. It was brought down by our artillery fire near Mons. It is the only one we have seen so far. The French Flying Corps does not appear to be doing very much work. The French General asked General French if our FC could get him some information as the French FC had not obtained any.

'Went up for reconnaissance at 11.30 with Major Moss as passenger [observer]. I could not get Henri to climb at first so came down and lightened the load, then we soon got away at 3,800 feet. We found the enemy very thick to the south-east of Thuin and a battle was in progress below us. The artillery on both sides were very busy. It was very interesting to watch. In one field a French battery opened fire; it had not fired more than two rounds per gun when shell after shell from a German battery burst over them. It must have been perfect hell for the French battery and silenced them at once. On the way back some German howitzer battery opened fire on us from north-west of Thuin. One shell splinter

passed through my left plane but did no damage. Some
infantry in Thuin also wasted a thousand rounds or so trying
to bring us down.

'*24 August.* All yesterday heavy firing to the east and
northeast, and it was apparent that the enemy was pushing
us back. I was sent off on to some high ground to look out for
zeppelins!! No. 3 Squadron—ours—left at 2.30 pm, landed
at Berlmont at 6.45 pm, then ordered to retire further back
to Le Cateau. A great rush to get off as it was getting dusk.
I and some others landed in a wrong field but went on to the
right one afterwards. Birch in his Bleriot hit the telegraph
wires in getting off and broke his machine, escaping with a
shaking himself.

'*25 August.* Yesterday the Germans had a victory at Mons.
Today parts of Charleroi are in flames and the enemy are
turning our left flank. I went off at 11 am with Jackson as
passenger. All our troops were in retreat, using every road
available and making for Le Cateau. The whole of the French
cavalry were retiring on Cambrai. Returned from reconnaissance at 1 pm and at 3.30 orders came to move to St Quentin.
As soon as we landed a heavy rain-storm came on and swamped
everything. I feel so sorry for poor Henri. It is doing him a
great deal of harm, this rain and hot sun.

'*26 August.* Off on reconnaisance at 7 am with Jackson to
report on engagements in the Le Cateau and Espignol area. The
whole sight was wonderful—a fierce artillery engagement for
the most part, we getting the worst of it. We had all the German
army corps against our little force. We could see nothing of the
French. I watched one of our batteries put out of action, shell
after shell burst on it and then there was silence until more men
were sent up and it opened up again.

'Le Cateau was in flames. We were shelled by anti-aircraft
guns so I kept at 4,500 feet. We are also giving the Germans a
bad time—their cavalry and infantry nearly always advanced
in masses, offering as they did so a splendid target and getting

mown down by the score. There was not a suitable place to land at headquarters at Bertry. In landing we skidded and as soon as we touched ground the landing chassis gave way and Henri pitched on his nose. Jackson was pitched out about ten yards ahead and I was left in the machine. Neither of us was hurt only shaken. Good old Henri, he did me well and even at the last he did not do me in. There was no time to repair the damage as shells were already falling over the town so I hurriedly removed all the instruments, guns, maps etc. and cut off the Union Jack and so left Henri in his last resting place.

'When we arrived in the town everyone was busy getting out of the place as fast as he could. At Headquarters General Smith-Dorrien spoke to me, asking me where I had come from, and when I told him I had broken my machine he was very kind and said "Well, you must not be left here, you are wanted with the Flying Corps", and then, like the sportsman he is, found someone to give me a seat in a staff car. I think we got away only just in time as shells were bursting all round the town. We went to Maretz where roads everywhere were crowded with troops retiring. It was not a good sight, the look of dejection and despair everywhere. Poor fellows, they had had no sleep or food for three nights and days, being driven back and pressed always by the advancing army. The Germans have us on the run and we are fighting a rearguard action against big odds.

'The situation must be rather a critical one for the whole of the BEF. A staff officer in the car that I was in went so far as to say that if the Germans pressed on hard now nothing could save a rout and the British Army being decimated. It certainly was not hard to see that we were in a very tight corner, with men, guns and transport blocked all along the roads. It was like what one has read in books of disordered retreats. Men were throwing away their kits. Some were carrying their wounded pals and nearly all the carts and limbers had wounded in them who could not be attended to through the hurry of the retreat. Here was a situation where discipline counts for so much. Where it was high, battalions and companies—what was left of them—were in some semblance of formation, but in units where it was not so high men straggled badly and the officers were coming along by themselves. There can be fewer sadder sights than a defeated army retreating.

'Well, thank God, although shells were bursting a mile away they did not come up to us when we were blocked along the roads to Maretz. The Germans were as dead beat as we are. We went on to St Quentin, stopping on the way for Jackson to give his report. I got some dinner in St Quentin and slept there. Was feeling hungry as I had had only a roll and cup of coffee this morning.

'*27 August.* Got up at 6 am and went off to find our camp but I heard they had flown to Nozons twenty-five miles back so went back to HQ in St Quentin, which was filled with troops marching through, and managed to find a seat in a staff car. At Nozons found the RFC was at La Faire twenty-five miles away. Also found some of our fellows with a car going there so got in. Pretyman and Waldron have also had accidents and broken their machines since I went away.

'*28 August.* Reveille at 5. Mist delayed departure until 10. Having no machine I went in a car to Compiegne. Still we retreat. What can the French be doing?

'*29 August.* Received orders early to go to Paris to take over a new Henri Farman. Pretyman, Wellesly, Abercromby and Major Brooke-Popham came in the same car, the first three also to fly back machines. We all lunched in Paris and then went over the Farman works in Paris, afterwards going on to Buc where the machines were ready.

'*30 August.* Dined this evening with about thirty officers of the French Flying Corps at the Naval and Military Club in Paris. Coming back to Buc in a car we were fired on by a

French patrol—the bullet just missing Pretyman's hand. German aeroplanes dropped bombs over Paris today.

'*31 August*. Lunched with several French Flying Corps officers at Versailles. Evidently we are still retiring. At this rate the Germans will be in Paris within a week. Orders arrived at 6 pm to fly at once to Juillie but we did not go as it was too late to get there before dark.

'*1 September*. News that the Germans are in Compiegne and the RFC are leaving Juillie. The British have been bearing all the brunt of the fighting and the French will not hold their ground although they are superior in numbers to the Germans. Can they be acting on a plan to draw the Germans on to Paris or have they really got their tails down?

'*2 September*. Received orders this morning to fly to Serris from Buc. Arrived at 12.30.

'*3 September*. A rather disastrous day. On coming back from reconnaissance I smashed my new Henri on landing. The engine "chucked it" at a critical moment when I was near the ground and about to go over some Indian corn. I tried to "pancake" the machine but as soon as the wheels touched we did a complete somersault. I was knocked out and Major Moss, the observer, had his back badly bruised. Everybody thought we were killed and I think we were lucky to get off so lightly. I got a broken nose and damaged knees. Poor old Major Moss, I feel such a brute doing him in through my own fault. The machine was absolutely broken up, including the propeller. I have broken up two machines in a week. [Major Moss had, in fact, fractured his spine and walked thereafter with a bowed back.]

'*4 September*. Feeling rotten today with a sore head and a pair of legs that ache. Did nothing until we had orders to pack up at 2 pm and go to Melun. No machine so I went in a car. We were given billets in a convent school. The place had of course been forsaken by everyone. I think the little ladies had left in a hurry as all their nighties and other things frilled with lace had been left behind. Captain Herbert looked ridiculous in a nightie much too short for him. We collected sheets and pillows etc from various places in the school. Herbert snores abominably.

'*5 September*. I was told to fly Fuller's old Henri No 274 to Etampes and, with mechanics who were sent by car, to take it to pieces and recover the planes. It is a big aerodrome with some sheds. The Germans are moving east and appear to be ignoring Paris for the time being. It seems to be the idea of the French, having brought the Germans round to Paris, to cut them off and round them up.

'*6 September*. Fuller, I and Birch found billets in Etampes at the house of a merchant who, with his wife and daughter, were as usual very hospitable. Dinner at the Hotel des Trois Rois. Fuller flew back to Melun this evening—I think he was sorry to go as he seems to have made several friends.

'*7 September*. Work on machine.

'*8 September*. News that we have driven back the Germans yesterday. They are now retreating as fast as they advanced. They probably are finding themselves in a tight corner. We are on their right and the French on their centre and left. Things are looking brighter than they were and our men have had food and rest.'

It was not until 14 September that the renovated Henri Farman was ready to take Read back into the fight. This was the day that the Germans reached the river Aisne after a five-day retreat from the Marne to begin entrenching themselves against the jubilantly pursuing Allied armies. It was the start of nearly four years of near-static warfare, trench facing trench, a ghastly war of attrition that Read, buoyant at the thought of the enemy on the run, could have had no conception of as he headed his tiny biplane the ninety miles to his bivouac near the Aisne.

'*15 September*. I flew over the east of Paris. The Eiffel Tower stood out very clearly and I kept well away from it as they have anti-aircraft guns on the top and fire at anything coming within two kilometres of it. Feel awfully glad to be up at the front again with everybody. We are well within sound of the guns here which keep up an incessant booming like thunder. A battle has been going on at Soissons where the Germans are endeavouring to make a stand in their rapid retreat. Three days ago we took thirteen thousand prisoners. Two days ago forty German officers were captured in a wood—they were all drunk if the story is to be believed. Three nights ago a sudden squall got up and turned over five BEs and two Henris. They were all badly smashed up. Shek's machine was making love to Fuller's—one was found leaning against the other.

'*16 September*. At 2 pm orders to do a reconnaissance north of the Aisne. At 4,000 feet the Germans opened fire at us with anti-aircraft guns and they made surprisingly good shooting for the first few shots. The first burst about twenty feet below us and I felt the machine shake and the left wing was boosted a little. I made rapidly for a thick white cloud on my right and as soon as I came out of it they were on to me again but the shots were wide.

'*17 September*. Flight to locate enemy batteries a wash-out because when we were getting our height at 3,500 feet we lost the magneto timing wheel and the engine stopped suddenly. We had to come down in the best field we could. This battle of the Aisne as I suppose it will be known in history has now been going on for five days. Each side is holding its ground. A large force of French cavalry is making a flanking movement round the enemy's right flank. If they get round in time it ought to alter things in our favour.

'*19 September*. It rained all last night and our bivouac, made out of two Henri Farman wings leaning against each other, did not altogether keep out the rain. This morning a brigade of Algerian cavalry—awful looking ruffians with khaki trousers and flowing red cloaks mounted on small lightly built horses— passed by. Two brigades of French Chausseurs also passed

31

going west to reinforce our left flank. Fuller smashed up Henri 247—the machine I was rebuilding at Etampes.

'*20 September*. Started off at 6 am, with Walker as observer, to fly over the 5th Division and receive orders from the divisional artillery officer. At about 10 am the sky cleared and we went off to locate a battery which has been causing our troops a deal of annoyance. We discovered the battery just as their anti-aircraft guns opened fire at us. Their shells burst all round us but we did not offer them a very good target as we were well above the clouds and only showed ourselves occasionally. We gave in our report to a major belonging to one of the 60-pounder batteries and went up again to observe fire. We soon got them on to the battery with the aid of Very's lights and our shells must have caused them a good deal of damage. Clouds came down and as we could do no more we returned to camp at 4 pm. This evening went out with Shekleton to shoot partridges—we brought our shot guns with us from Netheravon and everybody else is envying us as there are a lot of birds here.

'*21 September*. Yesterday the Germans attacked all along the line and were repulsed everywhere. They were making some headway on our left until the Algerian cavalry which passed through the other day attacked. It is reported that their war cries alone were too much for the Germans who turned and fled before the Algerians got to them.

'*22 September*. Reconnaissance with Jackson. Mapplebeck was shot through the thigh while chasing a German machine today. We have now only one Henri in the flight and are waiting for new ones to be ready. Went out shooting again this evening with Shek. We bagged $2\frac{1}{2}$ brace and a hare.

'*23 September*. All last night and today troops have been passing through to Soissons to strengthen our left flank and roll up the German right. At last we have had a fine day after three weeks of rain and wind and one has had a chance of drying damp clothes. The French cavalry horses are looking in very bad condition, they are losing horses all along the road. This morning I shot one with my revolver as he was too far gone to recover. Gave another water and grass to recover enough to get up and be taken away to a shed. Shooting with Shek—two brace and a pigeon.

'*24 September*. Flew from the 5th Division landing ground to report whether the Fort of Conde was occupied as it is thought it may be a general headquarters of the enemy. We came back to report that it was and it was decided to bombard the Fort with our four six-inch howitzers which have just arrived from England. They throw a shell of 120 lb, the heaviest we have. Went up again to observe results. Fire was deadly accurate, every shell falling inside the Fort, doing deadly work as far as we could see. This new Henri I am flying today climbs rippingly and gets up to 5,000 feet in under the half hour. It was brought in from Paris yesterday

'*25 September*. A day of mishaps. First the cylinder cut out and we had to come down. Then the engine missed badly and the Very's light pistol jammed. Down again. Then, all the while we were circling and observing the Fort, the enemy plastered us with anti-aircraft guns until the air all round was thick with shell bursts. I kept turning, diving and climbing but we lost height a good deal and, when at 3,500 feet, they managed to burst a shell near enough to put a piece of it through our propeller. So, having got our battery the range, we decided to get away and land.

'*26 September*. Day in camp. There is a ripping touch of autumn in the air now and we get light frosts in the mornings. The country looks beautiful in its autumn tints and war seems out of place among these ripping valleys and orchards. Went out shooting this evening. Bagged 2 hares and $1\frac{1}{2}$ brace.

'*27 September*. Church parade this morning. Shek and I went foraging in the countryside afterwards in a car for bread, eggs and milk. We are living in an old barn house and sleep upstairs on a stone floor with some straw laid down. Our table is an old barn door supported on sacks of corn. This evening Shek and I went out to shoot partridges. We only had eight cartridges but managed to bag five birds.

'*28 September*. On duty from 5 pm today for twenty-four hours to be ready to go up and chase German machines which may come over. Poor old Henri, he is no use for chasing Taubes, he is too slow.

'*29 September*. Stood by all day but none came over. I wonder how this battle will end. How long the war lasts depends a good deal upon which side wins this battle. As far as one can see it is likely to go on indefinitely. Both sides hold very strong positions, especially the Germans, and both sides are pretty well dug in by now. The losses would be tremendous if either side tried to drive out the other by a frontal attack. Probably a big turning movement is what will decide the battle.'

Read's assessment was partially correct. The battle of the Aisne simmered down into a solidified front and the bulk of the British and German armies moved north, intent on outflanking each other, to finally batter each other to a standstill in the bloody first battle of Ypres, culminating on 11 November.

Read was active most of this time, based at Amiens, Moyenville, St Omer, sometimes airborne in reconnaissance and plotting flights for more than four hours a day. He engaged in his first dog-fight with a Taube, chasing it with revolver shots to the German lines. He took in his stride the occasion when a bullet knocked a chunk off his propeller, which then parted company with the machine, taking with it half the engine nose plate on a solo trip to the ground. It was 'Archibald', the RFC's nickname for the German ack-ack guns, that began to tell on him.

'*22 October*. I notice several people's nerves are not as strong as they used to be and I am sure Archie is responsible. I would not mind quite so much if I were in a machine that was fast and that would climb a little more willingly. Today we had a good dressing down by Archie and some of the shells burst

Cavalryman in the Flying Machines

much too near and I could hear the pieces of shell whistling past—and they have to burst very close for one to be able to hear the shrieking of loose bits of shell above the noise of one's engine. Well, well, I suppose the end will be pretty sharp and quick if one of Archie's physicballs catches one. I think I would rather it caught me rather than crumple up Henri because one would have too long to think when falling from 4,000 feet.'

But it was in action with his squadron that Read was really in his element. He writes revealingly of four days in Paris, where he had gone with some others to fly back new machines.

'*17 October*. We put up at the Hotel Ritz because some kind individual, name unknown, is paying for billets there for officers of the RFC. I have a ripping room, double, with bath-room attached, which costs 50 francs per day in peacetime.

'*19 October*. Had dinner at Maxims and, wishing to be quiet, we went into a corner but the women would not let us alone and they all seemed to choose the same corner to come and have their dinner, and of course they wanted to talk. I feel such a chocolate soldier walking about this Paris in uniform with everybody staring at me. Every time we go into a shop we attract a small crowd. In some cases one does not mind as there are a lot of pretty faces returned to Paris.

'*20 October*. Another hopeless day for flying. I'm sure they will be thinking at St Omer that we find Paris too entertaining to tear ourselves away but personally I am sick of it and want to get away back to the front. Am staying at the sheds at Juvissy here tonight instead of going into Paris. The others have gone.

'*21 October*. Back at St Omer. Everybody is looking very mournful about something—or perhaps it is that I am feeling less mouldy after being in Paris.'

In mid-November Read was wounded in the leg by a bullet during a reconnaissance flight and, unwillingly, invalided back to England. In June 1915 he was back on the Western Front as a flight commander. In October 1916 he was in command of a squadron. Between spells in England and four months he spent

back with his regiment, looking for fresh excitement, in command of a Hotchkiss gun detachment, his diary indicates the increasing role of the aeroplane as a vehicle for bombs.

His ethical attitude to the bombing of non-military targets is summed up in a 1917 entry following a raid on Ghent during which, owing to a mechanical fault, he had to push off a 250-lb bomb with his foot. 'Now the probabilities are that it fell in a quarter inhabited not by Bosche but Belgians, and it seems to me that it is a merciful dispensation of Providence that my conscience does not accuse me of being a murderer. Thank goodness one's conscience is forgiven these things in war-time . . .'

In June 1918 Read was put in command of No. 216 Squadron of the recently-formed Independent Air Force commanded by General Trenchard, founder of the RFC. Headquarters were at Autigny-la-Tour, a picturesque village in the heart of the Vosges, within striking distance of industrial targets in Germany. But that these could be synonymous with the 'Reprisal Raids' many people at home were clamouring for is clear from an occasion Read records in his manuscript autobiography.

'On one occasion I had been to Cologne, which was a long 5-hour trip, and I felt tired on getting back. As soon as I had stopped the engines a deep, gruff voice came up from the ground: "And where have YOU been?" Feeling irritable, I said, "Oh, I don't know where the b— hell I've been." And then I recognised General "Boom" Trenchard and said I was sorry. "All right, all right," he said in his gruff voice. "Where did you go?" "To Cologne, sir." "What was your target?" "The Hohlenzalken Bridge, sir. But you might as well stick pins into a pin-cushion, sir, as bomb that bridge with 112's." "Did you hit it?" "Yes, several times, sir. But I am afraid one or two bombs overshot and hit the Cathedral." Then, in a muffled voice from "Boom", "GOOD." It was at that time that the Bosches were going for our most treasured possessions in London and I was all out for paying them back in their own coin. So was "Boom", but he could not say so officially.'

It was only the cessation of hostilities that thwarted Read of a cloak-and-dagger adventure that he would have relished and which would have established his name in Air Force history. There is no mention of it in the official biography of Trenchard by Andrew Boyle, though Maurice Baring briefly alludes to it near the end of his *Flying Corps Headquarters, 1914-1918*. Read's pencilled account in his last diary is the more dramatic for being interspersed with routine matters crowding in on him as a squadron leader as the war draws to a close.

'*7 November*. After lunch I went up to the General's room and he unburdened his heart to me. I am to take a flight of six Handley Page's to Bohemia, find a landing ground somewhere north of Prague and bomb Berlin from there. Having pinched a map off his wall and heard the gist of the scheme, I pushed along to start to make arrangements. Personnel and equipment to be as little as possible. As soon as I got back I started on making out a list of personnel of all trades required that I would want, pilots, observers, gunners, transport, spare parts and goodness knows what not. I am to be ready to push off in a few days time.

'The General rang up tonight to say that I am to go to Headquarters tomorrow morning at 10. Albrecht, who is Acting Wing Commander, came round this evening and was very annoyed at not knowing what was afoot but I, having been told to keep things profoundly secret, could tell him nothing.

'*8 November*. Had a very busy day going through all departments arranging what personnel, transport, spares, equipment, rations, armament and clothing we were to take. The affair seems to have created great excitement at IAF. They seem to regard it as a rather hazardous enterprise. Certainly I do not know what sort of reception the Czechs will give us. They do not like the Bosches but they are reported to be all split up into bands and there is a state of general revolution amongst them, so some may love us and others may resent our intrusion into their country.

'In the terms of peace we have the right to use their railways so I take it we shall be able to get up there all right. As soon as my train load of stuff is collected and packed, I, with the remainder of personnel who do not go by air, are to push off. We go via Trieste. I am taking six weeks' rations, 14,000 gallons of aviation oil, 600 112-lb bombs, £4,000 in money, 74 NCOs and men and 30 officers including pilots and observers, a medical officer and recording officer, 74 rifles, 104 revolvers, 5,000 rounds of revolver ammo and 60,000 rounds of .303 ammo. I stay out there until my rations run out or all my bombs have been dropped—whichever happens first.

'Machines fly over after I have arrived there and arranged an aerodrome for them to land on. My scheme for showing them where to land is for them to leave here one night five hours before dawn, fly via Strasbourg, Stuttgart, Nuremberg and Pilsen to Prague, a distance of 390 miles which they should do in seven hours. Soon after leaving Nuremberg it should be dawn and they fly to Prague in daylight. North of Prague I shall have a large arrow placed on the ground pointing in the direction of the landing field and by the side of the arrow the number of miles in Roman figures. At the actual landing field I shall have a large smoke fire burning and a large white circle of fifty yards in diameter.

'The whole success of the expedition depends on finding a good landing ground and getting machines there safely. It is a grand adventure and, if successful, will beat anything that the air force has done in the war. HQ have given me everything I have asked for today, including sou'westers for the men and gum boots, extra blankets, rum, fleece-lined coats, leather jerkins etc. We shall live in bell tents and of course machines will stand out in the open. Tonight Crossfield and Pring, the two observers going to Prague, went off to Paris to meet Colonel Gordon at the Paris office. Crossfield has gone since he knows the country and Pring because he can talk Hungarian and German ... Tea with Prince Albert and high-ups ...

'*9 November.* Have been very busy all day making out nominal rolls of pilots, observers, rear gunners and other ranks, also detailing the machines and transport. Lots of work on the telephone but tonight I have broken the back of it all. HQ are arranging a special landing party to get all stores on the train and I have nothing to do with that. I think it is certain that we shall not move from here before Monday (Nov 11th) night, we shall wait until it is known whether the Bosche have accepted our peace terms or not. In that way we shall be the first almost to know as they will certainly push us off at once if our terms are not accepted. In the same way if nothing happens by Monday night I shall take it that the peace terms have been accepted.

'A lovely day but a cloudy night and no Ops. were possible. The Kaiser is officially "out of a job", nearly the whole of the German Fleet has mutinied. Personally I do not think we shall ever get to Bohemia at all.

'*10 November.* Spent a busy morning in the office making final arrangements for our Bohemia trip. Visits from officers in various departments ... A mysterious message came in from Brigade this evening, which I could not understand quite. It ran as follows: "One machine to be got ready at once. One observer will be supplied you. One rack of Cooper's bombs will be carried. As much petrol as possible to be carried. Pilot must economise in petrol as much as possible. Submit at once names of remaining personnel." I did not know in the least what was required but I guessed it meant that the General wanted to bring off a stunt trip of one machine to fly to Berlin from here and land in Bohemia.

'I rang up Brigade and told them it was not possible to do it on the amount of petrol that a Handley Page carries, ie ten hours, as it is 650 miles to Berlin and then on to the Austrian frontier. However, thinking that another squadron would get the job if we did not accept it, I rang up Brigade again and said that it was a possibility and that I would be pilot in the machine with Harding as observer and Corporal Blakeman as rear gunner.

'News this evening that the Bosche have signed the terms of the armistice It is to be a 25 days armistice. Don't know what the terms are yet. It has not caused very much excitement with us yet, in fact everyone seems particularly quiet. I suppose we have not had time to assimilate the news yet. But I expect there will be a huge blind tomorrow night.

'*11 November.* First message in this morning was that no machines to get off the ground under any condition without Brigade permission. At 11.30 I got all the officers, NCOs and men together on parade and told them that they were expected to carry on as usual and keep up the reputation of the old squadron, no falling off of discipline, etc, etc. This afternoon the squadron's 1st eleven played the second XI at soccer and we got up an officers' team to play the NCOs at medicine ball. I played. We beat them three sets love.

'This evening I heard unofficially some of our terms of peace which the Bosches have accepted. I suppose our chances of going to Austria now are very remote indeed although perhaps we may still go so as to be able to start bombing Berlin at once if the Bosches do not stick to the terms of the agreement. Crowds of maps have arrived for me this evening from IAF for the Austrian trip . . . The Kaiser has gone to Holland also the Crown Prince.

'*12 November.* Last night WAS a night . . . Two officers have arrived from the Air Ministry in connection with the trip. One is an intelligence officer called Taylor who knows the country etc, and the other is also an intelligence and liaison officer who can talk the language, knows the Czechs and, if the show comes off, is to be flown over to Prague in advance to make arrangements re aerodrome and generally to promote friendly relations between us and the inhabitants.'

The show—a show to end all shows—did not come off. Apart from a passing mention that he met Taylor, the Air

Ministry intelligence officer on 19 November, Read makes no further reference to it in his diary. He plunges immediately into a meticulous record of the squadron's move to Marquiese in France, where it was temporarily employed to deliver mails to Cologne by dropping them by parachute. 'No more will our Handleys be used for the honourable purpose of war,' he rue-fully writes. 'We are postmen.'

In his handwritten autobiography Read refers only briefly to what might have been his greatest adventure. He describes it as a 'feasible proposition' and suggests that Trenchard was as sorry as he was that it did not come off. But he also suggests that it was perhaps just as well that that special train did not rumble across Europe on its mysterious errand and the six bombers land in that white circle in a field north of Prague.

'The armistice came,' he writes, 'and so fell through a very interesting trip which was destined, in all probability, to end in disaster. I say "disaster" because, of the two observers, Cross-field and Pring, only Pring returned and reported to the Air Ministry. Crossfield disappeared, Pring said, and nothing more was heard of him. It was thought that he had sold us to the Bosche.'

2   *Death Wish in No Man's Land*

Lieutenant William St Leger was 23 when he was killed in action in the battle of the Lys on 27 April 1918. A fellow-officer who survived the war wrote: 'We remember his eagerness to work, his keen sense of joy in all he did during 18 months of continuous service in France, and a coolness and gallantry under fire which were the admiration of all who served under or with him.' He seemed the epitome of that generation of death-defying young patriots enshrined by Rupert Brooke. But there was another side to him, a tormented side, hidden even from friends who shared the rigours of the trenches. It was confided to the diary he kept daily throughout this period and which has recently come to light.

As the war progresses and St Leger sees his friends killed one by one, the plain recital of daily events becomes tinged with an introspective soul-searching. He begins to relate his dreams, to ponder about life after death and to imagine himself reunited with his dead comrades-in-arms. '. . . They are waiting for me to join them and when I do will give me a great welcome. Then I will understand everything and be happy and content . . .'

St Leger was particularly shattered by the death in action (while he was on leave in England) of a young officer who had only recently joined the regiment. Denis Buxton was son of the Governor-General of South Africa, a brilliant old Etonian destined, his friends agreed, to be a future prime minister. It

42

was just after he learned of his death, in October 1917, that St Leger had a clear premonition of his own death in the following spring: a dream that came true.

Reading these transparently honest diaries is to enter a world it is difficult nowadays to imagine. It is a world where patriotism, dedication to a cause, devotion to duty and service to one's fellows have not become tired clichés. And the diaries reveal a world within that world, its kernel the platoon he proudly led, its perimeter the regiment, the Coldstream Guards —'the finest Regiment God ever made'. For the most part the diary is a straightforward account of happenings, but between the lines one senses that *esprit de corps*, that close companionship inspired by the sharing of hardships that by all accounts was the one redeeming feature of the war. Whether writing of men in his platoon or fellow-officers, 'love' is a word St Leger uses without embarrassment, echoing in a less articulate way the emotions that gave a new dimension to life to men like Wilfred Owen and Edward Thomas and Siegfried Sassoon.

St Leger would have been at home in that dugout portrayed in R.C. Sherriff's *Journey's End*—hero-worshipping and hero-worshipped. He is immensely bucked when he hears that his commanding officer ('a white man of the first degree, a FINE man') has described him as 'a GENTLEMAN', and quotes from a letter he has been censoring in a batch from his platoon: 'Corporal Lay says I am "a brick" and he also says other things which, though untrue, please a chap very much as they show one's men believe in and like one'. On leave in England he devotes more space in the diary to the visit he paid to a war hospital to see Corporal Simkin, who was wounded in the raid he led which earned him the MC, than to the ceremony at Buckingham Palace when the King hooked the medal on his tunic and he walked out 'treading on air'.

It was on this leave that he had a studio photograph taken 'to please Mother'. A still-boyish face, with firmed-down dark hair and a small moustache, gazes at the camera with the ghost of a smile. One feels this young man would look more natural sporting blazer and flannels than officer's tunic and Sam Brown, legs encased in puttees down to well-worn boots, one hand in trouser pocket, the other clutching a stout stick.

St Leger was born in Hertfordshire in 1895, son of Dr R. A. St Leger, and was brought up in George, South Africa, where his family had moved shortly after his birth. He had just matriculated at South Africa College, Cape Town, when war broke out and had served briefly with the Cape Town Highlanders in German South-West Africa before he came to England. He was commissioned with the Coldstream Guards on 5 May 1916, and arrived at the Western Front just in time to take part in the second Somme attack. The diary opens on 21 September 1916.

'We left the Citadel near Carnoy last night about 7 pm and reached here at 2 am this morning. This is the front line trench, about 800 yards south-west of Lesboeufs, which was dug on the 15th September after the Guards' great attack. We are 300 yards from the Hun. We are No. 2 coy of the 2nd Btn. Fildes and I are in a shell hole a few yards in rear of the trench. Fildes is OC Coy.

'It was a great job keeping the men closed up last night. The battlefield of the 15th is a ghastly sight. The ground is simply pitted with shell-holes, dead men lie here and there, heads towards the enemy, and nearly everyone lying on his face. The moon, peeping occasionally from behind the clouds, shines pitilessly down upon this treeless, devastated, god-forsaken land of the dead and everywhere is the stench, somewhere faint, somewhere strong. It all looks so sad and one thinks of all the homes to which those brave men will never return.

'McGregor and Cromie, with No 1 Coy, are on our right, 300 yards nearer Lesboeufs and across the road. Fildes went across to see them last night and says that three Huns came in and surrendered, throwing themselves on their knees and crying "Mercy, Kamerad!" Fildes said he had never seen such worms in his life and that if they are a sample of the people we are going to attack we should have an easy time.'

His detailed description of the ensuing action, like that of other battles he took part in, is imbued with a sense of excitement, the horrors underplayed almost as though it were some inter-regimental field day in progress.

'At noon we got ready to move off. About this time our barrage started, and the Hun retaliated. A great British aeroplane swooped down over the trench, Bosche shrapnel bursting all round it. It swerved and shot off towards the Bosche lines, quite low. The airmen ARE brave fellows! The barrage was soon an absolute roar, and the trench began to rock. Cromie produced his cigarettes and gave me one, I had unfortunately lost mine. Fildes sat watching the beetles making short disjointed rushes at the bottom of the trench. They didn't know what on earth was the matter.

'At 12.35, the time for the attack, we heard the devilish rattle of machine guns above the roar of the guns and knew that the attack had gone forward. The Hun barrage seemed to increase its roar. It seemed a marvel that no shell came into our section of the trench. A rocket went up from the Hun line. Cromie turned round and said happily "See the Hun SOS!" A message came down the trench: "First objective taken with very few losses." We went forward and filed into the vacated front line trench.'

The Grenadier Guards had stormed the village of Lesboeufs ahead of the Coldstreams, whose task it was to 'clear up'.

'The gentle Hun has a delightful habit of leaving machine guns and gunners in cellars after he has retired. These come up and attack the attackers from the rear after the village has been taken. Fildes and I each had a plan of the village and had given names to certain streets and houses, Piccadilly for the main street. The two largest houses with the strongest cellars we had named the Ritz and Berkeley. There was one house we noticed belonging to a Madame Bocquet which was marked

45

as having strong cellars capable of holding fifty men. We planned our call. We should go to the door and ring the polished bell. A neat housemaid would come to the door, and we should say "Is Madame Bocquet at home?" Housemaid: "No, sir, she has just gone calling." We: "Can you tell us if anyone is staying in the house?" Housemaid: "I believe fifty gentlemen are staying in the cellar, sir." Fildes (loudly to men outside): "Ten bombers in here. Sharp's the word." '

As it turned out, bombers with hand grenades were not required.

'Fildes said that the Huns had simply run for their lives when the Grenadiers came through the village, throwing away their arms and equipment in order to get away faster. Fildes had got a Lewis gun on to them and accounted for a good many. He saw three Irish guardsmen, out a couple of hundred yards in front of the line, hunting five terrified Huns with their bayonets. The Huns ran so fast that they only bagged one, and him they shot.'

St Leger's company went forward again next day.

'We went down a sunken road. Just round the corner we came upon some RAMC orderlies burying the remains of a party of Irish guards, amongst whom a Hun shell had fallen. The second sunken road we reached had a great many dead Huns and several dead guardsmen in it and they were lying all over the road. We reached the trench and commenced to get the dead removed from it. There were a lot of Hun dead in it and several dead guardsmen, including Lt Knachtsbull-Hughesen, MC. They were splendid men—great broad-chested, tall fellows with strong fearless faces, and it seemed such a pity. We got the dead removed outside the trench and consolidated it. The Hun was shelling our original front line and a little later turned his attention to us. A "Coalbox" dropped right into a firebay of the trench where two of our men were standing, blowing one to pieces and burying the other. He was dug out luckily unhurt.

'Fildes and I had a great time at lunch. We had no knives or forks, so used matches as forks to take apricots out of the tin of preserved apricots. I distinguished myself by drinking a mixture of port and apricot juice out of the tin—I have not yet acquired the taste for port alone.

'I selected a good Mauser rifle after we had done our work in the trench, and also two Hun bayonets and 60 rounds of Mauser ammunition in three leather pouches. These will be useful after the war, though I don't know how I shall get them to England, as I don't expect to return to England until after the war is over, as old Dad is at Marseilles and I want to spend any leave I have with him. I'll try and store it in France until the war is over.'

That night they were relieved by the Irish Guards and marched back to camp near Carnoy, arriving at 4.30 am.

'Whew! it WAS a great relief to be home again, with dinner and bed awaiting one. Fildes and I went into the mess and had dinner, meeting Shaw-Stewart there. He looked so clean and fresh and we must have looked like a couple of tramps, dirty, unshaven. The Colonel came in, rubbing his hands. "Hullo, hullo. HQ are awfully pleased with the division's work. They want us to do another attack. I don't mind the Battalion going in again, hang it, they have done so well!" We smiled ruefully and retired to the sleep of the just. The Battalion had lost all of its officers except two, and two-thirds of its men in the attack on the 15th, the other battalions of Coldstreamers even more heavily, and we did not feel like doing another attack.'

It is only in retrospect that the horrors begin to register.

'This was the end of my first scrap. When one looks back on it one thinks of the horrible sights we saw, which would have horrified us in civil life, and simply interested us now. I think the ghastliest sight was when we entered the front line trench after the attack had gone forward and found the damage just done by the barrage. An RAMC officer and some orderlies were already at work. A little further on we came upon a great broad-chested man of the Irish Guards lying on his back in a part of the trench half blown in. His chest was covered with blood and his head hung back. He was dead, and as each

man passed he had to tread on his chest. The weight compressed
the corpse's lungs and the dead Irishman groaned and gasped as
each man passed. I would not tread on him but managed to
jump over him. Just round the corner was another Irishman
sitting down on the side of the trench and bending forward.
The top of his head was blown off and his brains were dripping
over on to the ground in front.'

At a rest camp during the next few weeks St Leger is shocked
by news of the death of two fellow-officers, Cromie of Number
1 Company and Lt Basil Christy, whose obituary notice he
quotes: 'Aged 19, educated Cheam and Eton, President of the
Eton Society, played in the eleven in 1914 and 1915, was keeper
of the Field and had his Fives choices.' 'Poor old Christy,' he
writes, 'he was such a great sportsman, a dare-devil motorist
and afraid of nothing on earth. It seems such a shame.' After
receiving a letter from Christy's mother—'such a nice grateful
letter, but she seems heart-broken, he was only a boy, and his
life was so full of promise'—he attempts to formulate his
philosophy on the war and the future. Coming from a man
brought up in South Africa, its racial undertones, with emphasis
on the Yellow Peril, read oddly today.

'I hope to God the politicians in England will not betray us
and make peace before we have absolutely crushed our enemies,
and made a repetition of this hellish business impossible. To make
peace before this is done would be a criminal betrayal of the
Living and the Dead. Modern war is hell, and we must make
a recurrence of it impossible for all generations, cost what it may.

'The Yellow Peril will of course come inevitably some day,
but the White Races of the world must never again be engaged
in this suicidal business. Hundreds of thousands of brave men
have still to lay down their lives, leaving ruined desolated homes
to mourn their loss. But over the graves the armies of Right and
Civilisation will sweep invincibly on. If only the sulkers and
imitation men in various parts of the Empire—thank God they
are only the small minority—could pay the great bill of human

life, instead of the real men whose blood would enrich the nation and posterity, but this cannot be. War is ever the survival of the unfittest.

'It is a war of exhaustion and battles now are more massacres than warfare. The white races are losing millions of their finest men. But there is absolutely no alternative. Perhaps those who survive will be so much ennobled by war that they will make up for the loss of the great Dead. But until our enemy is absolutely crushed, peace is utterly impossible.'

It is difficult to gauge how far St Leger was influenced in his thinking by what he had read in newspapers and current publications and by the general climate of opinion around him. He records 'ennobling' poems that have appealed to him (one by Denis Buxton) and on one occasion alludes to the padre giving a 'great lecture on what we are fighting for'. His only other reference to the padre is when he one day 'borrowed one of the padre's horses for a hare hunt'. His descriptions of camp life are mainly concerned with the trivia of the daily round—lectures, parades and exercises, entertainment in the Mess, camp concerts, the gramophone grinding out the latest hits—'High Jinks', 'When maiden loves, she sits and sighs', 'The Spaniard who blighted my life'—and sporting events— hunting, shooting, cricket, football, boxing, wrestling on horse- back, four-handed chess . . . There is a boisterous public school air about it all that makes the more chilling the knowledge of what lies over the horizon.

'. . . Catch phrase in the Mess is "You CAN'T do that here!", introduced into the conversation whenever possible and always makes us smile. The other day Anderson, Kirk and a couple of others came trotting up the High Street at a great rate. Feilding and Porritt met them. Feilding got into the middle of the road and signalled to stop them. When they had all reined up to hear his news, he said 'You CAN'T do that here!" . . .

'Great dinner tonight when Bumble, Symon, Scotty and a Grenadier, Simons, were the guests. The company became

49

very noisy later on, attracting in most of the officers of the Battalion. Fraey brought in his Hun skull. He says when he found it, it was wearing uniform and he scraped off the flesh and hair. Ugh!! I don't think it is quite the game and I should think a souvenir like that would be bound to bring bad luck . . .

'Bill Lundie got hold of a cricket bat and started playing French cricket and made everyone roar with laughter. Rail and Lutgens had an "Oxford and Cambridge" boat race on the canal. Rail could only go half the pace of Lutgens as his boat, being the detachable stern, had no proper bow. A barrage was opened on the leading boat . . .

'Henry, Porritt and I went to the "Lillywhite's" revue again—really splendid. Was glad to see that Cinderella had learnt to refrain from the horrible act of taking off her wig to sing the National Anthem . . .

'That idiot Penfold put my boots in front of a fire to dry them yesterday and simply baked them—they cracked up when I put them on. I gave £3 for these boots five months ago so I feel rather sick about them. Wished I could have stuck to Howard for my servant—"an absolute gem" . . .

'Charles Hambro and Longworth filled in a sandbag and also a rum jar with ammonal and exploded them in the hope of making the army in this part of the world believe that the Huns were sending over some more 112 shells. They succeeded in their object and "put the wind up" three RASC men with wonderful success . . .

'I got hold of a Mills bomb this evening, took out the explosive and put in a cap and a fuse with no detonator. I put it in Thwing's bed under a pile of clothes. He had spent the day in Amiens and came in and lay down. He put his head on the bomb which started fizzing. Thwing was the only one who heard it, as it was under his clothes, but he thought it was the air escaping from his air pillow. So it fell rather flat . . .'

But all such goings-on were incidental to the serious business of preparing for the next spell in the trenches and the moulding of his platoon into 'the finest in the Regiment'. A grim sense of duty underlies his description of one route march back to the front. 'Broiling hot day and a lot of men fainted on the line of march. One or two had fits and made a horrible row. I dropped back to try and get some of the men round. Last halt only 300 yards from farm billets. About twelve men remained there when we moved on, absolutely unable to move. Some piled groaning unconsciously into a car, rifles and equipment piled on top of them. One man groaning and unconscious did not look as if he would last much longer. We got hold of the doctor who told us he was afraid he seemed as if he would not live.' Two days later St Leger reports: 'Five hours route march in full marching order for all men who fell out. Those who were not unconscious when they fell out have also got eight days CB. It seems hard but this is war and everyone MUST march until he drops.'

A week in November 1916 that St Leger spent on leave in Marseilles with his father, who was senior major in the South African Medical Corps, is tersely recorded, as though his thoughts were elsewhere. Tea at club, dinner at Mess, Sunday Service in the English church, train and motor trips around the Riviera. At a variety entertainment in Nice 'the principal lady singer threw a pink flower at us and hit Dad on the chest. I pointed out to him that he should get up and say a few words but he did not seem to think it was necessary.' And in Cannes he met a doctor's daughter. 'She was a charming girl and very pretty, looking something like Cecile Burnett, only perhaps daintier. She said they wouldn't allow her to nurse in the hospital as she was too young, but she did want to do something for the war. All British girls want to be "doing something". They are splendid. I had not met an English girl since I left England except nurses at the chateau at Camp Mussot, and they are hardly what I term "girls". She is a Miss Bailey . . .'

Shortly afterwards he was back in the line with the first snow falling, prelude to a winter of agonising cold.

'All the bodies out in front of our trench turned white. These bodies are a ghastly sight. One had been torn in half by artillery fire. One body lay on its back with its face facing the enemy as if the poor fellow, mortally wounded, had propped his head against something to watch how the others fared ...

'*Xmas Day*. The Army has orders to shoot at sight should the Hun want to fraternise and come across. Sgt Hepple says a Hun suddenly stood head and shoulders above the parapet, took a drink from a bottle, held it out towards the sergeant and got down again. Tonight I went out wiring. Suddenly some fool in our support line sent up a Very light and there we were in the limelight twenty-five yds from the Hun trench. We lay flat but the Hun had seen us and fired. We jumped into the sap head, but my foot got caught in the wire and there I hung until Sgt Harris managed to help me out. Awful moment—expecting that beastly machine gun to start any moment ...

'*New Year's Day*. The night was pitch black when I went on duty at one o'clock. I very much wanted to know what the men think about this peace talk, so I asked a sentry, Robinson in my platoon, what he thought about it. The answer was what I had hoped for and thought he would say. "I don't think we can have peace now, sir," he said. "If we don't beat them properly we'll have to fight them again in a few years time."

'*17 January*. The snow lies thick upon the ground this morning. The poor devils in the trenches must have had a hard time last night. Gamble very likely there ...

'*19 January* ... I dreamt the other night that I was in a beautiful place, evidently somewhere in England in spring, and Gamble and I were walking slowly over a green field beside a hedge. The night before last I dreamed I was standing in a trench which was being heavily shelled. I dreamt a dud fell a foot in front of me, two more duds tore my tunic and an aerial torpedo fell next to me, also a dud ...

'*24 January*. Last night at mess the ginger ale was frozen. We thawed some a bit but when we poured it out it froze into the glasses. The perrier water froze as soon as we opened the bottle. A little ginger ale spilled on the table and froze there. Two oranges this morning were as hard as cricket balls ...

'*17 February*. Last night dreamed that Henry Feilding and I were in a post made of poles and sacking in a line of similar Hun posts. Somehow you couldn't shoot through them although they were only made of sacking. Not knowing how to eject us the Hun sent some ladies to come and talk to us who, while carrying on an interesting conversation, worked the sacking off the poles. We saw the danger too late and, rudely ignoring our fair callers who retreated, began to put the sacking back again. The two neighbouring Hun posts were only five yds away but we remembered to our joy that a kind of truce existed and the Hun did not shoot. Then the Huns began to throw bombs over. We searched our post and found to our dismay that we didn't have a single bomb or any ammo. Eventually we managed to get an artillery barrage from our guns on each side of the post. We lay on the ground vainly hoping for a Mills bomb to silence the Huns, then woke ...

'*26 February* ... Buster hit. If only we could always be with each other in danger, I mean all everybody's friends and stand or fall together, but it is the fortunes of war ...

'*19 May* ... The hills are yellow with dandelions and buttercups. I looked at one buttercup plant particularly and it struck me as being so familiar, as if I had known it in bygone days, and yet it was so beautiful and wonderful. I think thoughts like that are reflections of thoughts and actions cast back from childhood days. Jenny and all of us used to play among the buttercups and daisies when we were very small, made daisy chains and held buttercups under our chins to see whether we were fond of butter. Now we live in a world where everyone is living solely to kill his brother man ...

'*22 May*. Felt very happy marching behind a drum and fife band. "There's a long, long trail a-winding, Into the land of my dreams ..." I have been marching that long, long trail now for more than two years. The trail winds and doubles back

53

on itself. One thinks "Here I walked with Buster", "Here Gamble and I stood in that trench at night and watched our barrage straffing the Hun trenches opposite ", "Here I walked with Gerrard O'Brien when the snow was on the ground and the frost intense" . . .

'*25 May.* Rode to the Military Cemetery at Grovetown. Christy's grave has yellow and violet pansies growing on it. Someone has put a small cross of carnations on Butler's grave— I suppose it was his mother. Afterwards we rode into the valley of the original Grovetown and back home past copses and some beautiful glades. We passed a hedge with several May trees in it. The scent was beautiful.'

On 9 July St Leger writes in detailed length about the bombing raid he directed, with forty-five men, over a canal to the German front line in the Ypres salient. Its object, in preparation for the forthcoming British offensive, was to discover in what strength the trenches were held and the identity of the division, believed to be new to the line. The password was 'Thistle'.

During the raid Corporal Simkin of St Leger's platoon was shot through the right abdomen. 'I asked him where he was hit. "In the upper part of the leg, sir," he replied, polite as usual. "I think I was shot by one of our own party by mistake, sir," he added. "At the corner I tried to say 'Thistle' but could only say 'Th- Th-' and could not get the word out. Then he shot me." ' St Leger describes how Simkin stretched out his hand from the stretcher on which he lay and beside which he was kneeling. ' "Goodbye, sir, I'll write and tell you how I get on." "Do—do," I answered, gripping his hand, a lump rising in my throat. I had always loved him, but I did not know how much till then . . .'

'*16 July* . . . I dreamed I was holding a trench on a desert island by myself. Suddenly I saw three men coming down the trench. I thought they were Corporals Owers, Meekings and another man, so told them to halt as I was not sure in case they were Huns. They came on so I told them to halt or I'd stab them with a bayonet which I held in my hand. They still came on so I stabbed them. They gave a hollow groan and I recognised them. They looked at me reproachfully and very gently and I was shocked at what I had done. Then I woke up and my servant told me that Corporal Meekings had been wounded.'

On 31 July began the third battle of Ypres, to become known as the 'battle of the mud', which culminated on 7 November with the capture of the ruined village of Passchendaele, at a total cost of some 300,000 British casualties. St Leger's company spent the night preceding the initial attack in the corner of a field near Boesighe, north of Ypres.

'Too cold to sleep. Cheerless breakfast in thin wet mist at 3 am, the eggs and ham were all cold and I upset the coffee. I was very sorry but no one complained at my carelessness. We had some tea which, with thick condensed milk, was rotten. The rum was the only good thing, which I dislike, so I did not partake.

'Zero was at 3.50 am. There had been firing all the night but at that moment every gun began to speak. The whole horizon to the north-east, east and south-east was lit by one continuous dancing flame composed of jagged flashes of bursting shells. The guns made a deafening row. The solitary broken walls of a ruined village with its shattered spectre of trees showed up grimly against the blazing horizon. Sgt Harris gave a short laugh: "A fine picture of civilisation, sir!" he said. "Fritz's Reveille," said another.

'We passed across the next field where No. 4 Coy had spent the night. It was still dark. Suddenly Bumble appeared. "Good luck, Bill," he said, gripping my hand. "Thanks, Bumble," I said, gripping his. I met Henry a few yards further on. We wished each other good luck. I said I'd come and have tea with him at Crapouillots Wood that afternoon. Soon after we moved forward. The Huns were shelling the canal with 5.9s so I felt I should be pleased when we had got across. However I did not lose a man there. Two very young German

55

prisoners passed us on their way back just beyond the Steam Mill. I could not help smiling at their youth. One of them smiled back! On either hand as far as the horizon one saw men moving in artillery formation. It was a glorious sight.'

St Leger, who was 'camouflaged in Tommy's uniform' (a precaution taken by officers at this stage of the war to prevent them being singled out by enemy snipers) and who had picked up a dead Grenadier's rifle and bayonet to supplement his revolver, led his men from shell-hole to shell-hole behind a creeping barrage and dug in at 9 am under heavy shellfire. 'Went across to Grenadiers on right. I found half a dozen who asked for permission to shoot a Hun inside, who was terribly injured and had, they said, been asking them to shoot him. I did not like the idea, but while I hesitated Judge came along. I asked the German in my best Dutch whether he would like us to shoot him, but he said he could not understand and waved his arm from east to west. I thought he meant his pals would come and eat us. "He wants to be taken down," said Judge, "don't shoot him." '

St Leger's platoon remained dug in, in full view of the German gunners, for some hours ('a hedge near us seemed to be eaten up in chunks by the shells'). At one stage he went to confer with the neighbouring platoon officer, leaving in charge Sgt Harris, whom he had earlier described as 'the best platoon sergeant in the Regiment'.

'Came back and to my dismay saw a fresh body lying just behind the hedge. I turned him over. He was Sgt Harris. He was warm and unconscious. He groaned. The right side of his face had been blown in, and his neck was cut and bleeding. I got the stretcher bearers and they said he was done for, as his jugular vein was cut. The blood was coming out in a steady trickle. I thought it would have spurted out but they knew better than I.

'At 3.10 pm a shell burst thirty yards away and a fragment came over the parapet and hit me just above the knee as I was

sitting in the trench. It felt as though someone had hit me with
a heavy hammer with a knife attachment and that my foot had
been driven into the ground. Corporal Pritchard cut off the leg
of my trousers and bound it up. I found I could limp along and
went to battalion HQ.'

From there he was given a lift by an officer in a Daimler to
the dressing station where he was inoculated. 'I did feel a rotter
going down, but thought I would not be of much use up there
with a lump of iron in my leg.' When nothing was found in the
wound he insisted he should rejoin his men, but was finally put
on a train to Boulogne, thence to Le Havre.

On 19 August St Leger rejoined his battalion at a reinforce-
ment camp. 'Saw my MC in Divisional Orders. Found our
Mess where Judge, Billy and a stranger were dining. That was
one of the happiest moments of my life. The stranger was Denis
Buxton, an awfully nice chap. We sat and talked till very late.
Buxton, who is mess president, got me some dinner and offered
to lend me some clothes until mine arrived, as my valise had
been sent to Boulogne. It was an offer which I gratefully
accepted. Dozen letters for me, one from mother enclosing
fine poem by Denis . . .'

The friendship that blossomed in the next few weeks is
barely indicated in the diary. St Leger refers to a long talk
about South Africa in their tent at night. On 24 August
Buxton volunteered to go back with him to the Ypres battlefield to disinter six of his men from the shell-holes where they
had been buried, 'between Captain's Farm and the Green
Dotted Line', and rebury them beside three officers behind
the farm. On 25 September, after a visit to his father at Rouen,
St Leger writes: 'Good to be "home" again. I went for a
stroll with Denis. I wonder if this is the dream I dreamed
of walking over a field with Gamble come true. Perhaps it
wasn't Gamble, only someone of whom I was very fond.
The field in the dream was sloping and this one was flat
but the hedge on the right was there and the little stream

with the trees beside it which we crossed at the entrance to the field.'

It was the last time he was to see Buxton. Next day he went on a ten days' leave to England. He spent some of the time with his sister Jenny, a nurse at the South African Military Hospital at Richmond, visited other relations, joined parties for dinner and the theatre (the Gaiety, *Chu Chin Chow* at His Majesty's), went to the dentist and his tailor, had his photograph taken. He also called on the widow of Sergeant Harris and 'told her all about him', and took a taxi the fifteen miles from Northampton station to the military hospital at Kettering to see Corporal Simkin ('he seemed very glad to see me and very pleased about my MC').

The day before he returned to the Front, his two closest friends, Henry Feilding and Denis Buxton, were killed in the Ypres salient, Feilding by shrapnel from a British barrage, Buxton while leading his company in an assault. 'I was told Denis was delighted at the prospect of going over the top. "Won't St Leger and Butler-Thwing—those two professional parapet-poppers—be sick when they find what they have missed and we have gone over when they haven't." I lay thinking about Denis a long time before I fell asleep. I felt very unhappy and kept speaking to him, half expecting him to answer me. It was a wet, windy night.'

There is a week's gap, the only gap in the diary, during which St Leger was back in the line. It resumes on 21 October.

'Jimmy after dinner seized my diary while I was putting on another record and pretended to read it and we had a great rough and tumble before I could get it back. I do miss old Denis so, Henry too, but Denis more. I feel I would give anything almost not to have gone on leave. I have been pretty miserable without him. When I shared a tent with him I used to wake up in the morning and feel my heart glow with happiness to see him sleeping peacefully at the other side of the tent. Then I used to get up and exhort him to do the same. When I went up the line I felt that I wouldn't mind a bit if I did not return. I wanted to be with him again—with him and Henry and Porridge and all those other good fellows who have gone. But I believe that everyone comes into this world for two purposes. 1. To do a certain work. 2. To fit himself for a better existence. When he has done these two things I believe he is taken away to God to enjoy his rest. I wonder when I shall have fulfilled my part. But still,

> Is life worth living? Yes, so long
>   As there is Wrong to Right,
> To help the Weak against the Strong
>   And Tyranny to fight.

'But meantime Denis and Henry and all those others are happy together—supremely happy and MUCH happier than I ever was when I was with Denis, and they are waiting for me to join them and when I do will give me a great welcome. Then I will understand everything and be happy and content. Denis was the first friend I had that I absolutely loved who I felt returned all my affection. Oh, if only I had not gone on leave, but nothing can recall the past, so it is no use worrying or being unhappy about it. But I feel I have lost interest in everything.'

Buxton's body was not found.

'Corporal Ronson told me that he found Denis lying in a shell hole, he had bled a tremendous lot and had slipped down into bottom of hole up to his waist in water. Denis simply said, "I'm hit, Corporal Ronson." He told his men to go on, and Corporal Ronson pulled the piece of shell out of Denis' neck, bandaged the wound and made him comfortable against the side where he could be seen and yet under cover and went on. The coy reached its objective without any officers and dug in. Cpl Ronson sent a man back to look for Denis, but could not find him. He had passed the first objective and had gone altogether about a thousand yards when he was hit. If ONLY I could have been with him.'

Later in the diary St Leger mentions letters he has received from Viscount and Lady Buxton, enclosing a copy of the order of service at a memorial service in Pretoria Cathedral. ('Lady Buxton said that when her brother-in-law in the regiment was killed Denis said he thought it was an ideal way of dying, to be killed in action with the Coldstreamers fighting magnificently.') There was also a memorial service at St Martin-in-the-Fields in London ('Mother's grandparents were married there') and an obituary in the *Eton Chronicle*:

> The Hon D. S. Buxton came to Mr Well's House in September 1910 and was captain of the House and a member of the 6th form when he left in the summer of 1915 to visit his father in South Africa before joining the Army. It is hardly possible to say how much he was loved by his friends and how deeply they will feel his loss. He combined the highest intellectual ability with a great personal charm and in the world of politics which he intended to enter after the war there was no distinction to which he might not justly have aspired and the most brilliant future seemed to lie before him. His life, alas, has been cut short but it was full of happiness—a happiness which he unconsciously spread among all his friends who will never forget his high ideals and his noble character.

St Leger also copied out a poem by Buxton, published in the *Westminster Gazette*, entitled 'A Plea for War'. The last verse reads:

> We that are young, how shall we then complain
>   Of so much gain?
> For Friendship never were such days as these
>   In times of ease;

There never were such days as these to scan
  The God in man—
And praised be war, if only that it brings
  Rest from the weary strife with little things.

The last two dreams recorded in the diary are dated 28 October 1917.

'I dreamed I met an ensign of this regiment who told me that he would be killed in the spring. Then I saw myself what was going to happen. This battalion was holding the line and the Germans attacked. They got into the British trenches and were just in front of a shattered village and killed every man except about a score who managed to hold out in one portion of the front line trench. Then from the air above the village the spirits of the officers and men of the regiment who had been killed swept down through the ruins of the village into the old British trenches and drove the Germans out. I suddenly realised that I was the ensign and my spirit was one of the spirits who drove the Germans out.

'I was with the company in a front line position at dawn. There was no wire in front of the trench and it was quite new, evidently dug during a British push. Behind me was the old German pillbox, half buried in the ground and next to it a shell hole full of stores and salvage. Suddenly in the morning mist I saw a man walking towards me about 150 yards in front. Then on his right another and a third and fourth and many more. It was a long line of Germans extended to two or three paces intervals. "This is an attack all right," I thought. I turned to Pte Harrison who was looking for something in the shell holes of stores and told him to pass me the SOS. "I am just looking for it but I can't find it," he said. I wondered why the Lewis guns and machine guns didn't open fire. I thought: "It seems to me that I've got to repel this attack by myself."

'An enormous German about 8 feet by 3 feet broad was coming straight towards me. When he was about ten yards

61

away I fired my rifle at his chest. But he must have been wearing a new kind of steel waistcoat for the bullets glanced off. The line of Germans reached the trench. I presented my bayonet point at his chest as he stood on the parapet but it glanced off. "Ah, your bayonet is too blunt!" he said. I thought "My number is up now. I hope he will shoot me rather than bayonet me." Then the dream ended. Half awake and half asleep I thought to myself that I was going to be killed next spring. For a moment I felt sorry then I didn't seem to mind, thinking that I should have finished my work on earth and I should meet Denis and Henry and all the others.'

Between the premonition and its fulfilment lay the battle of Cambrai which St Leger writes about at length with all the old sense of excitement and *esprit de corps*, as though in violent action he found release from the ghosts that haunted him. This was the historic battle in which Britain's top-secret weapon, the tank, was first used on a large scale to forge a way ahead for the waves of infantry. The Guards Division was among nineteen divisions of the British Third Army engaged. On 20 November 1917, 381 tanks led the attack, the 'impregnable' Hindenberg Line was smashed and a wedge some five miles deep and four miles wide was made through the German lines over the rolling chalk downland east of Cambrai.

After news of this spectacular advance, victory bells rang for the first time in the war in London churches. But prematurely. Within ten days the Germans, who had quickly rushed up reinforcements, had regained nearly all the ground they had lost. War historians have blamed the generals for failing to follow up the chances offered of a complete breakthrough. An official court of enquiry held at the time put most of the blame on the indifferent powers of resistance of the troops, many raw newcomers to the front line, when the Germans counter-attacked on 30 November. It was this stage of the battle in which St

Leger was involved and his account gives some backing to that judgement.

At 10 am on 30 November, St Leger's battalion received news that the Germans had attacked very heavily at dawn east of the village of Gonnelieu. The battalion moved at 11.15 am.

'We marched down the road passing men without arms and equipment walking back towards the village. They were the 12th Division, we found afterwards, who had broken and given way before the Hun attack. "Look at them, sir!" said Drill Sergeant Brittain. "Soldiers, sir! SOLDIERS! 'Ardly CREDITABLE, sir! To think that British soldiers could do a thing like that, sir!" We passed our Brigadier standing by the side of the road smoking a cigarette, notebook in hand. We found afterwards that he was taking the names of everyone of the 12th Division going back and heard that he had put 1,500 under arrest.

'The battalion formed up in mass beside a wood behind the brow of a hill. The position was this. The Huns had advanced and occupied the high ground west of Gonnelieu and had pushed their outposts forward into Gouzeaucourt. The battalion was to advance, drive the Huns out and seize the high ground beyond. Nos 1 and 4 companies were forming the front wave and 3 and 2 were in support. We were supporting No 4. "Good," I thought, "I'll be supporting old Butcher in the battle." It was all just like a field day. "We have got open warfare at last," I said to Sgt Battrick.

'As soon as the leading companies went over the brow of the hill they came under machine gun fire. We fixed bayonets. We passed a trench just this side of the brow of the hill held by a machine gun company of a line regiment. Our men joked and laughed with them as they passed. Several hares got up and ran about everywhere to the men's huge delight. I saw Gillie lighting his pipe. There were a lot of cavalry following up on our right some distance behind. We went over the hill deploying into line on the top, under fire the whole time. We saw the Germans on the hill running in front. "Do you see them running?" I said to Howard whom I saw next to me. The men were all smiling and laughing "Do you see Fritz running?" "Look at Fritz running!"

'We sorted ourselves out a bit at a line of dugouts half way up the opposite hill and then went forward again. When we crossed the brow of the hill we came under very heavy machine gun fire indeed, together with a hot fire of 5.9 shells. We started advancing in short rushes. A 5.9 shell plumped into the middle of my platoon, followed by another. One man's torn body went hurtling over my head and dreadful groans came from where the shells fell. I shouted out to the platoon to advance, to get them on before more shells came. Some men of the line regiment who had appeared on our right started running back. I shouted out to them to halt, but they took no notice. I pulled out my revolver and very nearly shot at them, but I thought it wouldn't do any good, as they all had their backs to me so would have thought that anyone hit was hit by a German bullet. If I ran after them my men might think I was running away. So I took my men on and found a subaltern of the line regiment advancing with about ten men. "Can't you rally them?" I asked. He said he thought they would return. I went on.

'We went on about half way down the hill, where there were some limbers and a badly wounded German. He must have been hit by the aeroplane fire. We had not a single gun to support us as all the guns had been captured or taken back, so two or three aeroplanes had flown in low over our heads and fired at the Huns as they advanced. They had used tracer bullets. I found I was bleeding from a small cut below the right eye. There seemed very few left of 7 and 8 platoons. I got them into some holes which had been dug in the ground and then went to the left to see what had become of the rest of the company.'

It was decided that, in their disorganised condition, they should sit tight until orders were received. St Leger went back to the remnants of his company.

'I saw Butcher sitting on the grass behind a trench. A bullet had gone through the fleshy part of his left leg just above the ankle. I asked him whether he could walk all right and he said he could and that of course he would carry on. He said it felt just like a hard hack at football. I had noticed that Firbank was carrying a rifle and bayonet so had picked up one too. I gave it to Butcher advising him to carry it, as if we advanced the Huns would try to pick off the officers. He would not take it but I said there were a couple of wounded men not far behind and I would get one of theirs. I had a great job to make him take it, as he would not take mine and said, "No, really, I'll be very angry if you make me take yours." So I pushed it into his hands and went back and got one of the wounded men's. It seemed so strange to be sitting on the grass with Butcher with a face like a girl's in the warm afternoon sunshine, with those strange bees humming round. My heart had gone out to him when he refused my rifle. 'Oh I do HATE to see men wounded," he said in a distressed way. "Can't we do anything for those fellows?"

'I went back to the two wounded men and managed to get one upon my back and put him in a trench. The other was shot through the stomach. He was in great agony and implored me to shoot him. His face was turning grey and I could see that he would not last more than a couple of hours. He said he could not stand it any longer and clutched at my revolver holster, begging me to shoot him. I felt very tempted to, but I thought I had no right to do so. I told him he would be all right and that we would get him back as soon as darkness fell. I tried to get some morphia for him but neither Butler, Peck nor Butcher had any.

'A good many Huns came running down the far hill towards us but we didn't fire much as we wanted to save our ammunition till they got closer. Suddenly a man said to me "There's a tank, sir!" A tank came crawling slowly over the hill. Others followed. The Huns began barraging with 5.9s. One tank caught fire and stopped. The Huns made excellent shooting practice on it. St Leger was more impressed by a cavalry charge he witnessed shortly afterwards.

'Some hundreds of them galloped hell for leather from the right across our front about 500 yards away. We were left in peace for a moment as the Huns turned all their machine guns on to the cavalry, emptying about a quarter of their saddles. They galloped back into a hollow, dismounted and attacked on foot, turning the Huns out of a sunken road.'

In the early morning mist next day, with only about half the battalion left, St Leger watched the Grenadier Guards attack towards St Quentin ridge. They had decided not to wait for the twenty tanks that had been promised them to spearhead their attack in place of a barrage.

'The tanks appeared at about 8 o'clock, one and a half hours late for zero. Peck suggested they should be given five extra attacks or some such punishment. The Grenadiers had met very heavy fire just inside Gauche Wood. They lost every company officer except one. I heard that poor old Guns had been killed. He staggered into a shell hole where Harry was sitting with a piece of shell aimed at the tanks through his left breast. He stretched out his hand and said, "Goodbye, I'm done", and sank back dead. "If only the whole of the British Army was as good as the Guards Division", I remarked to the sgt major. "I wonder why some British divisions are so good and a few so bad." "Oh better led, sir," he said. "If all the army were like the Guards Division we'd go right through." '

St Leger writes with his usual meticulous eye for detail about the confused activities of the next four days in and out of the fluctuating line. At one stage he enlisted the aid of the cavalry officer in command of the 20th Hussars ('a delightful chap, a short, stout, active fellow, a typical English country gentleman') in rallying and 'practically taking command' of three companies of the Middlesex Regiment. On 5 December the battalion was relieved and marched to Metz. The corps commander sent a message expressing 'to all ranks of the Guards Division his high appreciation of the prompt manner in which they turned out on the 30th November, counterattacked through a disorganised rabble and retook Gouzeaucourt, Quentin Ridge and Gauche Wood.' On 12 November St Leger writes: 'I found this evening a tiny piece of shell in my face—almost three-quarters of an inch below my right eye, where I found my face bleeding on the 30th.'

Life went on. That Christmas he dined at the Headquarters Mess. 'Lively long-range artillery duel—Rivington started throwing nuts but these were ruled out and preserved figs and pieces of paper were the missiles. Everyone wore paper caps from crackers. After dinner everyone had to stand on the table and sing or tell a funny story . . . Letter from Mrs Heeley—she is very brave about her husband's death. She says "Whilst on leave my husband spoke often of you in terms of admiration for he said he felt he could follow you anywhere . . ." '

On 28th December he went on two weeks' leave to England. He mentions that he is reading *Tom Brown's Schooldays* ('I like "little Arthur's" vision of death so much'). On New Year's Eve he looks back on 1917. 'It brought me promotion, honour, the greatest happiness and the greatest sorrow of my life. It has taught me many things—one thing being to look up and to realise that life on this earth is but a minute and miserable part of one's Life. It has made me think.'

But his investiture at Buckingham Palace on 8 January was still an occasion to be cherished. Once before he had saluted royalty—on a road near Ypres on 27 June 1917. 'We saw a very young Grenadier captain with several ribbons coming along the road. "Isn't that the Prince?" I asked. "Yes," said Porritt. "Sure?" said I. "Yes," said he. So we put our sticks in our left hands and saluted as we passed. The Prince returned the salute with an air of "This IS a bore. Why salute me?" '

Meeting the Prince of Wales's father was a very different matter. ' . . . We advanced very slowly one behind the other, through two large rooms with beautiful and large oil paintings and not much but beautiful furniture. The King was in the third room. The King hung the MC on a hook on my tunic put there in the ante-room, held out left hand as had hurt his right.

Coldstream officer read out "Lt William St Leger, Coldstream Guards". "What battalion are you in?" asked the King as he hung the medal on the hook on my breast. "Second, sir," I replied. "Second," said the King. "Very pleased to give a Military Cross." I did not hear him speak to anyone else. Wilks said he asked him to which battalion he belonged, but that he did not hear him speak to anyone else. He spoke to us I suppose because we are Household Troops. I walked out treading on air.'

On 17 January 1918, back at the front, St Leger was asked whether he would like six months' light duty in England, as he had been longer in the battalion than anyone else. He thought it might be his 'duty to Dad and Mother' to accept, but rumours of a German offensive in the spring decided him. 'I could not run away and leave my friends to face that while I enjoyed some soft job in England.'

From the trenches, on 30 January, he writes: 'It was a beautiful still night, there was no moon at first and millions of stars were shining. As I gazed at them I kept wondering if Denis and Henry were in any of them, though I thought not, and longed to see beyond them.'

The daily entries grow shorter. Training, lectures, assault courses, lead up to the battle of Arras, launched on 9 April. The last two entries read:

'*26 March*. March to Henu past retreating Aussies and 51st Division, up hill through lovely woods beyond Pas, full of wild daffodils. Passed VERY young signaller officer riding along. Thought what a child he looked.

'*27 March*. Marched fifteen miles and slept in our old front line. We are going in to hold the line so I am sending this back.'

3   Slaughter on the Somme

'It was a time one can never forget. At a Casualty Clearing Station one realised the meaning of war more than anywhere else. One could go and see all the country round Trones Wood and Delville Wood spitting fire from our huge guns and see the great crumps from the German artillery bursting amid indescribable wreckage and desolation, but here were gathered together the results of it all in broken humanity. I don't think there is any part of the human body I have not seen wounded, frequently blown to pieces.'

So the Rev John Michael Stanhope Walker summed up his experiences as a hospital chaplain during the battle of the Somme. He was addressing a gathering of fellow-clergy in England a year later, but the horror was still fresh in his mind. 'In those three months I buried up to 900 who had died in the CCS. We have had 1,300 in twenty-four hours, one night 700 came in after 11 pm. Sometimes one was in the moribund tent practically all day and night dealing with those who were given over to die or whose wounds were too numerous to deal with when so many others were waiting attention.'

In the battle of the Somme, which lasted, officially, from 1 July to 16 November 1916, the British lost some 420,000 casualties, the French 200,000 and the Germans 450,000. On the first day alone nearly eight times as many British troops were killed or wounded as in the battle of Waterloo. Death and mutilation on such a scale can scarcely be envisaged. But in the 'news-letters' Walker sent home daily throughout the battle, often written in the early hours of the morning in a state of exhaustion, cold statistics become flesh and blood. In the extremity of suffering all men became equal—officer or private, Christian or Jew, British or German. For Walker the inspiration to carry on his ministrations amidst the frightful carnage was the incredible courage displayed. 'No one could ever forget the lesson those men taught one, half blown to pieces and they suffered in silence.'

Walker was 45, seemingly a typical pipe-smoking, sporting padre, attuned to the old school tie as much as the dog-collar. Son of a Nottinghamshire rector, with four public-school-going brothers, he was educated at Repton and Brasenose College, Oxford. His son Jack, aged 16, was at Marlborough College, Michael, aged 11, at The Old College Prep School, Windermere. He was rector of Kettlethorpe, Lincolnshire (population 400), when he volunteered for the Western Front and came out to the 21st Casualty Clearing Station near Corbie, at the junction of the rivers Somme and Ancre, on 4 December 1915. In the seven months he had been there before the battle of the Somme, when casualties rarely numbered more than 300 at any given time and there was no desperate rush to clear the wards, there had been leisure to get to know many of the patients and to suit his ministrations to their individual needs. 'The wounded man is wax,' he wrote, 'he wants to talk about religion and frequently about his sins.'

During the height of the battle, with 'hundreds waiting, dozens dying', only cursory contact was possible. Though Catholic, Nonconformist and Jewish chaplains had been brought in, the bulk of the wounded professed themselves C of E, and Walker was engaged in a constant round of confessions, administrations of Holy Communion, absolutions, blessings. Even for one entrenched behind High Church dogmas and rituals, it had already been a disturbing experience to

discover how far short the front-line soldier fell from that heroic
Valiant-for-the-Truth so often conjured up in public school
chapel or parish church. In the months before the battle he had
been particularly dismayed by the steady stream of patients to
the hospital's isolation camp who had contracted venereal
diseases, including 'old offenders who often sought to justify
themselves' and 'a sadly large proportion of officers, some of
them completely broken, others more callous than any of the
men'. 'I do not want to strike a hopeless note,' he told his
fellow-clergy, 'but it is undoubtedly true that, apart from the
fear of death, there is not much that makes for Christian living
among our soldiers now in France.'

Throughout most of the news-letters, designed to circulate
among his family, Walker maintains a buoyant note. But there
is a hint of the intolerable strain in his description of a violent
outburst of horseplay in the officers' mess. From the blood-
reeking wards and the cries of agony he finds refuge among the
flower-beds and vegetable plots he lovingly tended. And it
is to such reassuringly civilised pursuits, to a quiet country
parish, that he returns at last, feeling himself defeated. 'Tommy
does not want religion. I don't persuade him.' — *P14 - YBI*

The 21st Casualty Clearing Station was converted from a
partly burnt-down motor-car factory, its grounds dotted with
huts, marquees and tents. Its function was to provide immediate treatment for casualties from the nearby front line before
they were moved by ambulance train or specially fitted barges
down the Somme to base hospitals at Rouen, Le Havre and
elsewhere. The staff of 95 included 6 surgeons, 3 physicians, a
dentist, 8 sisters. The countryside around was undulating and
beautiful. Nightingales sang in the woods that early summer.
Then . . .

'*Saturday, 1 July*. 7.30, the heavens and earth were rolling up,
the crazy hour had begun, every gun we owned fired as hard as
ever it could for more than an hour. From a hill near Veils over
us to left and right great observation balloons hung, eighteen in

view. Aeroplanes dashed about, morning mist and gun smoke obscured the view. We got back for a late breakfast and soon the wounded by German shells came in, then all day long cars of dying and wounded, but all cheerful for they told us of a day of glorious successes. They are literally piled up—beds gone, lucky to get space on floor of tent, hut or ward, and though the surgeons work like Trojans many must yet die for lack of operation. All the CCS's are overflowing.

'Later. We have 1,500 in and still they come, 3-400 officers, it is a sight—chaps with fearful wounds lying in agony, many so patient, some make a noise, one goes to a stretcher, lays one's hand on the forehead, it is cold, strike a match, he is dead—here a Communion, there an absolution, there a drink, there a madman, there a hot water bottle and so on—one madman was swearing and kicking, I gave him a drink, he tried to bite my hand and squirted the water from his mouth into my face—well, it is an experience beside which all previous experience pales. Oh I am tired, excuse writing.

'*2 July*. What a day, I had no corner in the hospital even for Holy Communion, the Colonel said that no services might be under cover, fortunately it was fine so rigged up my packing case altar in a wood behind the sisters' camp. Then all day squatting or kneeling by stretchers administering Holy Communion etc. Twice I went to bury, of course we used the trench we had prepared in a field adjoining. I first held a service of consecration, when I turned round the old man labouring in the field was on his knees in the soil. I buried thirty-seven but have some left over till tomorrow. Saddest place of all is the moribund ward, two large tents laced together packed with dying officers and men, here they lie given up as hopeless, of course they do not know it. But I can't write, I am too tired and I have some patients' letters.

'*3 July*. Now I know something of the horrors of war, the staff is redoubled but what of that, imagine 1,000 badly wounded per diem. The surgeons are beginning to get sleep, because after working night and day they realise we may be at this for some months, as Verdun. We hear of great successes but there are of course setbacks and one hears of ramparts of dead English and Germans. Oh, if you could see our wards, tents, huts, crammed with terrible wounds—see the rows of abdominals and lung penetrations dying—you meet a compound fracture of femur walking about—in strict confidence, please, I got hold of some morphia and I go to that black hole of Calcutta (Moribund) and use it or I creep into the long tents where two or three hundred Germans lie, you can imagine what attention they get with our own neglected, the cries and groans are too much to withstand and I cannot feel less pity for them than for our own. Surgeons and sisters are splendid and I go and bother them and they come without grumbling. But one cannot drag them away from lifesaving to death-easing too often. Now 4 am, the Jewish chief rabbi has joined us.

'*4 July.* The guns still pound away with fury, a heavy thunderstorm washes the dust of crowds a bit. Several evacuations, one of Germans, make our numbers more reasonable and the surgeons will get a good sleep tonight.

'*5 July.* It would be interesting to tell you all the tales that wounded officers etc tell, but that would not be allowed. All are very cheerful, though we are paying a terrible price. Don't be misled by English papers which publish hysterical headlines. Work slacked off a bit towards afternoon but there is much more in the air and we have evacuated by barge or train every possible case, so the decks are clear for another great influx.

'*6 July.* Ordered to evacuate all and make the most of an opportunity for a night's sleep. I have seventy-odd addresses still waiting for letters, so I should like a quiet day or two. We actually dined at the farm today, quite a treat but judging from all accounts shall not do so again for some time to come.

'*7 July.* This constant heavy rain will be serious for the crops very soon, it must also interfere with the movements of troops, the boots of the poor wounded are thick lumps of mud. Chief Rabbi Adler is quite an interesting man to have in the mess and is quite as much at home quoting and discussing from the Gospel or Saint Paul as the Old Testament. He has an officer son.

'*8 July*. Not very many in as we evacuate two or three times a day but the neighbouring CCSs have a matter of thousands. Our Corps has not been in it so much, it is a ding-dong battle, we take and they take back—the English papers are absurd. Many officers think it is fizzling out into another Loos.

'*9 July*. A glorious day at last. All night through the trot of horses' hoofs. The Push disorganises my services. Matins alone in my tent as none came. Evensong, four and self—how one misses services, we evacuate too rapidly to get any patients and as convoys of wounded are coming in at all times the staff are all busy. We get a lot of frightful wounds, loads of abdominal, chests and heads. No one can imagine what it is unless they come and see it. Will one ever be able to think of anything but mutilated dying men again, even outside among the flowers the groans of the unconscious and the involuntary cry of pain resound. Yet the silence of the sufferers is wonderful.

'*10 July*. Two evacuations but filled up as soon as emptied, and tomorrow we expect a rush. If only we could get a slack time for a bit I could get out to the trenches, I want to get into the German trenches very much.

'*11 July*. Over eighty officers in the night and several hundred men. We may move forward any time the Surgeon General says. It will be sad to leave the garden a blaze of colour, peas and beans just coming in and tomatoes and marrows doing grandly—I get much praise for my garden now, if I am not any other use I am some cabbage grower and why need ambition soar higher?

'*14 July*. A crowded day, only time to minister to the dying and to bury. One officer, Captain Kelly of Windsor—Bell Farm, Clewer Hill—to whom I gave Holy Communion was shot through the head and out at his eye, could not see out of the eye left, yet all he seemed to care about was thank God I managed to land safely for the poor observer's sake. How he brought his machine down blinded and in awful pain is a marvel. Lungs, abdomens and heads—till one says thank God when a chap says both thighs smashed and a hole through the right arm and two fingers off the left hand. I must say the diminution of head wounds is wonderful since the issue of the steel helmets, though ugly they are better than the French ones and infinitely superior to the Germans'.

'I am. It is awful to feel incompetent, there are tents, huts, wards all with their rows and rows of stretchers. One goes here and there—night is not a time for ministrations, you wake the few asleep to new agony if you are not careful, a few words, a few prayers, and how grateful they are and how bravely they suffer, the writhing form fighting with his blanket, the tortured face alone betrays what is going on. Then there are the delirious, of course there is noise, but they are generally together. Giving drinks is dangerous, a cup of cold water may bring excruciating pain to the patient, one has to enquire where are you wounded? and you get all sorts of answers— "everywhere but in my face" cheerily said one officer, then one helps to take out a dead man from the packed line, or give an extra blanket or pillow to prop a shattered arm or leg. The officers I think are most to be pitied in a rush, they are in their line of stretchers all accustomed to attention when sick or even wounded on an ordinary occasion, there ought to be someone giving morphia to the bad cases that are not being likely to be dressed—but what can you do? they are all at it, the day and night men alike. At 12.15 the surgical specialist who has been at it all day unceasingly asked me to wake him at 2 am.

'*15 July*. A crowded day. Many officers, some battalions have none left. One learns to move among the dead and dying with jests on one's tongue for the sake of the living.

'*16 July*. Still they come and still they die. Twenty-seven deaths today. Papers have to be very carefully gone through

75

before their things are sent home or a great deal of unnecessary pain could be caused. The news continues good, don't be too bucked, it is only an advance on a very small front, like Verdun, one hopes that it is part of a greater strategic move. Most German prisoners are well fed and well clothed and confident of victory. I should think I administer an average of twenty Holy Communions per diem. With some it is difficult eg today one man had no underjaw, chin and all blown clean away. The South Africans are very fine and hard. Some Indians are also fine, I wonder if they are hard, there is a hothouse sort of look about them.

'*17 July*. Tell Wilfrid I was talking to a Captain Hughes-Hallett today—badly wounded, he has played cricket for Derby and played against Repton and Notts. I also wrote to his father in Derby. I apologise to all for failing to write, I really have so many letters every night that I do not get to bed till 2 or 3.

'*18 July*. Many communions to dying, especially South African Infantry, they are fine men and straightforward, knowing their lives have not been clean they are ready to make their confessions. A good many gassed men came in, a new and very deadly gas, some died, already they look very bad, blue and their mouths full of froth. An officer described it to me, for five hours a stream of shells came whistling over in the dark— on striking the ground the gas was turned on, they were in fact gas cylinders, so there was silence but for the hissing of the cylinders flying over to do their deadly dirty work.

'*19 July*. Still they come car after car, the great quad of the factory is choked with them and then the shattered bleeding wrecks are taken out, four stretchers from each and the whole place is a shambles and the papers talk glibly of all the successes. It is good to keep people bucked up, it is good for *Punch* to put in that ripping cartoon of congrats to the New Army, but it is good to remember the cost.

'Sometimes the surgeons are represented as hard and callous, it is not true—daily I witness acts of mercy outside the surgeons' duties which a hardworked surgeon will steal away from the table to perform. But what am I writing? You will think I am valuing human life far too high or that I am getting depressed. I don't value human life higher than the Creator did when the strongest instinct he planted in the human nature was the instinct to preserve his life. And I am not depressed, I am sure that you would marvel and reprove me if you could see and hear the jokes and tricks which we perform in the mess, or you could see and hear the jokes one employs to cheer up that rare phenomenon, the depressed or over anxious patient.

'*20 July*. The guns never cease, English, French and German. The latter have brought up many and great reinforcements. The garden is very bright with flowers now, the first row of peas is ready, the huge pods are much admired by the blood-stained warriors. Green tomatoes have formed and small marrows, we have had some very nice carrots.

'*21 July*. The wards look packed with a very bad lot. It is a good thing not to be too squeamish, the smell of septic limbs and heads is enough to bowl one over. As usual a good many deaths, one had the back of his head off, another from his nose downwards clean gone. But it is the multiple wounds that appear worst, men almost in pieces, the number intensifies the horror, we get so few slight cases.

'At meal times I relax a bit—it keeps one going. When I got to dinner I found the old jolly fat quartermaster leaning out of the window. I stole up and emptied a large mug of water clean in his face from outside, I went in, he had got a syphon, I took hold of a doctor and held him in front of me, of course he got it and was furious. I hurled him at old Jackson and went round the table where twelve officers were seated, Jackson pursued, syphoning, they all got it and all rose up. I still dodged, upsetting chairs and men till there was pandemonium, the Interpreter and the Rabbi got a good soaking. Jackson and I then drank all that was left of the soda and the others had to go without it.

'*22 July*. It is quite difficult to get a moment for making up one's burial returns, writing the labels for the graves and letters, in fact one does not get to it till 11 pm and then one feels one ought to be round the wards but one must sleep a bit for this Push looks like going on indefinitely. Old Sir Anthony Bowlby, Surgeon General, is very much struck with my flowers and he says he will have me mentioned in despatches for the size of my beans and peas. A padre has come in gassed and one was killed yesterday, if there are a few casualties I may get a move, I think I ought to, one ought not to be too long at this job. It is so overwhelming, my proportion is so big—the other three chaplains had three between them today. I fall asleep when I sit down to tea.

'*23 July*. Evensong with two orderlies and four patients with minor ills but all lying, yet we sang psalms and hymns till the hospital thought we had a crowd and the gassed padre was homesick for his Leeds parish.

'*25 July*. An easier day. There is a rumour that the push is over and the line cannot be broken here, it would be awful if true because of the terrible loss of life we have endured. Been chatting with son of Elliott, the headmaster of Halifax Grammar School. The British Tommy is as thougthless and wasteful as they make 'em, he says, he costs his country as much as ever he can, if there is a nice bit of corn in a field he tramples it down instead of keeping to the path, waste and destruction mark his footsteps wherever he goes. And he is not a handy man, he seldom can tie a bit of string so that it will keep tied.

'*26 July*. A lot of generals etc over to inspect, great compliments about the garden. We have had to clear the decks for action, so as I hoped the rumours of a failure are nothing, still it is a terrible struggle and not what the English papers make out. We are not the best fighters, it is no good shutting our eyes to the fact. I was talking to a wounded barber from Hamburg today, I fear he and several other Germans are dying, he showed me such a nice family group, two very jolly little boys.

'*27 July*. We are moving steadily forward and the Bosches are really becoming a bit demoralised, surrendering more easily. We had a good many gassed men, also a lot more Germans. All our men and officers who have been in Mesopotamia and Gallipoli say that it was play there compared to here.

'*29 July*. An Oxford boy, so earnest in prayer and preparation for HC, so delightful in talking about his fiancée—am I going to die? I hope not for her sake—you know how we used to have our fortunes told for fun at Oxford, palmistry, well they told me three things, which came true, and now at this age I was to have a severe illness but I should recover. Poor boy, I expect he has belied his hand by now, when I last saw him he lay as dead asleep, pallid as the sheets, too bad for operation, femur and abdomen. After communion he said you've not got to go just yet have you? I said no, so his two hands took mine and he closed his eyes. I scratched my nose, he smiled and took my hand again. Next time I succeeded, he has not woken since and probably won't. They are all so grateful for the least little attention and so glad of what one might call unofficialism. They have been through so much, they do not seem to fear death— "What's your religion, old chap?" you say to one. "C of E" says the patient. "Why d'you ask? Am I going to hop it?"

'The garden is really gorgeous and the sides of the tents are down so the patients just gaze out at it. It is not easy to keep things decent though. The dogs all root up one's best, the kittens box the dogs' ears playfully and scoot into the flower beds and of course the tribe of huge dogs follow.

'*30 July*. Lord Northcliffe came with a lot of visitors, said it was the prettiest spot he had struck in France and asked who did the gardens. 1.30 am. Just been round tents and wards dimly lit by hurricane lamps, hundreds of cases you can't imagine it. Off to the officers, find a fine young fellow white-lipped and blue, help him to examine his past, suggest sins, yes no no yes and so on, why not confirmed, would you if you got better, yes indeed, eighteen months here have taught me something, you don't see things in the same light here. Then the main features of HC are sketched and eagerly he seeks to make the words his own—"Yea though I walk through the valley of the shadow ... for Thou art with me"—oh, the earnestness of such communions, just absolution, sometimes Humble Access—reception and peace, the hand laid on the hand for absolution, the X for blessing. Then into the officers' reception tent, jolly greetings, anyone of the Ox and Bucks? Hello, is that you Tommy? cheero, cheero etc etc. Round more wards and prayers to soothe a sufferer here and there, generally six or seven earnest Amens startle one coming from neighbouring stretchers one thought were asleep.

'*17 August*. Officer said "No padre, I am not as bad as that, I am not dying"—"well, old chap, I did not say you were, but you never know how these wounds turn out". "I shall recover, I feel I shall not die, but oh why can't I enjoy rest now I am here, why do I feel no interest in the things round me? Yes, I will recover and enjoy life again—gasp—are they attacking again?—now sergeant major—gasp—" (silence whilst I pronounce the committal) —two or three gasps—I call up the sister, his pockets are emptied and his body carried out.

'*19 August*. It was rather funny to go into the officers' reception tent and see three Scotch on one side and three Germans on the other and to hear conversation in French, bad on both sides. The question asked by a Scot was "Why do you hate the Scotch so much?" which caused the Germans much mirth. They call the Scotch The Women of Hell. It is a humorous sobriquet from several points of view, the pipes harmonise with the idea too. A good many died today with my hand on their heads. Of course one is so much accustomed that it does not affect one's nerves or anything of that sort, but it keeps coming over one like a wave, the madness and folly of it all. Will the day come when men of all nations refuse military service, leaving the Rt Hon Gents to scratch each other's eyes out?'

In the news-letter of 24 August one can sense the relief and grim curiosity with which Walker took a day off from his harrowing daily round to pay his first visit to the battlefield where it had all been happening—a countryside reminiscent of Wiltshire with rolling chalk downland, deep wooded valleys and scattered hamlets. In the still-bitter fighting of recent weeks the British had driven the Germans from some key positions on high ground. Chief of Staff General von Falkenhayn had been recalled, and had been replaced, on 23 August, by Hindenberg and Ludendorff, whose first act was to order the construction of the 'impregnable' Hindenberg Line. For Walker the tide of war was merely something that could be seen now as he cycled with a fellow-chaplain towards history's bloodiest battleground.

'Oh what sights, the multitudes scattered over miles and miles, the immensity of war as it now is was revealed as one looked over miles and miles of teeming multitudes, at night the fires everywhere gave the impression of a vast city. Left bikes and tramped past our old front line, through the former No Man's Land and oh what an absolute scene of destruction, miles and miles of country battered beyond all possible recognition. German trenches pounded to a mass of earth and barbed wire. Huge mine craters made a miniature lake and mountain district. Here where bricks and mortar are freely mixed with mud is Fricourt, there where gaunt boughless trees stand splintered is Mametz. So we wandered on, clambering over desolation, our nostrils assailed by smells which warned us of the unburied dead and our ears by the ceaseless roar of artillery, for this desolation literally belched flame from every corner, a vast area packed with artillery, lines and lines of guns, 12 inch howitzers and 9.2 naval guns roaring continuously on all sides, like huge tethered monsters straining at their chains, they leapt into the air as they recoiled, grimy gunners grinned as they rolled up their huge shells.

'The Coal Boxes which Fritz sent back sent up huge clouds of black smoke on all sides. Overhead the aircraft literally swarmed—forty at one time and twenty-something balloons, but they were far behind us. Bosche shrapnel dotted the sky but did not flutter the graceful sailing of these man birds as they signalled to direct the gunners. It was a relief to leave the garrison artillery region and approach the field guns, the GA shells screaming overhead to the long line of smoke ahead where their shells burst.

'The most wonderful things we saw were the German dugouts down long flights of steps or inclined planes, forty feet down, they lived defying our artillery. All through the winter when we were losing hundreds he was comparatively secure. Those three rows of comically painted dummies did for Tommy Atkins to shoot at, but come down and see Fritz's abode, passages carefully boarded like a Swiss chalet inside, timbers neatly morticed —telephone wires along the walls, you can hardly hear the roar of the guns—oh what an ingenious foe we have—that cosy little room, neat bed, carpet on floor, papered wall, iron girders carefully boxed—woodwork all done in varnished paint to match the wallpaper and beautifully beaded in darker shades—ceilings white, the essence of comfort, he did not mean to turn out of this. Above in the upper storey so to speak were windows, the glass of which had wire netting IN the glass to prevent it splintering.

'Outside auriculas, shrubs and roses in tubs—window boxes and flower pots—I cannot describe all the wonderful heating and ventilating contrivances. However we did kill him, as the Bosche burial grounds show, now all shell holes and not a cross unsplintered. But now Canadians had appropriated some of his best dugouts and were quite at home. Daylight began to fade, so we tore ourselves away from scenes of thrilling interest. We abandoned rifles we had picked up, they were heavy and so common.'

Back from the battlefield to the 'results of it all in broken humanity', Walker continues with his ministrations, his jovial attempts at boosting morale, but it becomes apparent that he is now haunted by a sense of inadequacy.

'*25 August.* I was giving communion to a chap, after the blessing his hands went together, eyes closed and he said "Gentle Jesus meek and mild, look upon a little child etc"—God bless father, mother, grandfather, and make me a good boy—then the Lord's Prayer. Being fair he looked such a little child—dear innocent boy, I don't think he will be alive in the morning.

'*26 August.* They have a wit in the officers' ward who keeps them all roaring, he reels out funny stories and my great friend who has four or five wounds, any one of which would kill an ordinary man, nearly bursts his stitches with laughter. I told him and he shrieked it out—I say, you fellows, I bust the stitches in a man's abdomen by that story of the Scotchman. They were all howling with laughter but the moment I knelt down you couldn't hear a sound.

'*27 August.* I buried the Kaiser today—got 'im at last—Pte A. Kaiser, he was so cheery about the chaff he got yesterday. I think I came across the record case for horror this morning—I spare you—strange to say, he still lives.

'*28 August.* One fine fellow, never known a day's sickness, grips one's hand, it is a week since he had Communion, can he tomorrow? So there is a little help preparing, he may not last, he is fighting to live for his mother and there are a host of friends he is going to win for God. One has to promise to come again before night for hand holding, how absurd it sounds but you can't help it—generally you have one on each side and you kneel between the beds for evening prayers.

'But I always feel if I tell these things dear people say Oh how splendid, isn't he cut out for the job? that's the trouble, he isn't. Or, doesn't he do good, see letters of relatives, especially officers. No, it amounts to this—one has an opportunity, the war is putting them into your hands so to speak, what am I doing with them? Far less than the average priest would do—I can swear to that. I am not any good at this sort of thing. I can't help them clutching at any straw and clutching me. And the multitudes one never sees, all the hut cases. Some die in the huts but I can seldom get in to them. And letters—I don't write one in ten that I ought. Why write this then? yes why! so say I. What does it all amount to? That I shall crawl back into my hole and leave this to the more efficient. Good night.'

Walker carried on until December when the battle was over,

patients were numbered in hundreds rather than thousands and the hospital was settling down to its old routine. There were far fewer cases now of the wounded man 'wanting to talk about religion and frequently about his sins' and even the unhurried Sunday services he had so missed at the height of the battle do little but underline a prevailing apathy.

'No, it is not worth staying out here whilst one has children at home. Tommy does not want religion, I don't persuade him. I give out there is a service and offer to conduct it and out of about 500, 200 of whom can walk, about a dozen come to Matins and same to Evensong. They would come as a favour to me if I pressed them, at least some would, but what is the use. They don't kneel when they come unless I ask them.'

Between the lines of the newsletters one can sense how Walker now yearned to escape back to the peaceful, predictable life of a country parson, a life he was to pursue until his retirement in 1946. One of his last letters, with Christmas in the air, has a chilling air of unreality about it. It echoes the note of near-hysteria with which he had earlier described the kind of involuntary horseplay that 'keeps one going'. He had supped full of horrors but had learned, at what cost to his spiritual resources one can only guess, to 'move among the dead and dying with jests on one's tongue'.

'We are children in the Mess, air balloons I got from Harrods are a constant delight. I damaged the old Quartermaster a bit by sending him flying on to a stove. One alighted on Ferguson's cigarette and he could not have been more scared if it had been a Mills bomb. Then ping-pong is vigorously indulged—bridge, of course, and patience. I took an air balloon into a ward where no sister bosses and there were howls of delight as they banged it down from stretcher to stretcher. It seemed sure to burst when it landed on the face of a chap whose face was like a squashed tomato, then it would settle just at the foot of a stretcher just out of reach of hands, but it did not rest, up went the leg, splint and all, and it was flying again.'

4 *Tommy Atkins, PBI*

'Not a tree, not a blade of grass, not one living green shoot, not a bird, not an insect—one vast stretch of pulverised and poisoned earth and mud. No one can imagine such a place unless they had actually seen it. The effect on you was worse than shelling or fighting, although you had that as well. Will power alone kept you going. Once lose that and you were finished.'

This description of the Ypres Salient comes from a 50,000-word journal, entitled 'A Few Tales of 1914-18', found by a North London antique dealer while he was sifting through lumber in the attic of a house in Wanstead in 1971. It is written in a firm, flowing hand in a 165-page, stiff-backed exercise book, and contains copies of sketches made at the Front—'Passchendaele, Germans just the other side of the two stumps', '12 o'clock midnight, Ypres, outside our cellar on aeroplane guard', 'Early Tank, knocked out and bogged down', 'Menin Gate— you passed through here from destruction to desolation' . . .

The author's wartime identity is meticulously inscribed on the inside cover: 'Ernest A. Atkins, 26699. B. Company. 16th Kings Royal Rifles Corps. 33rd Division. 100th Brigade. 4th Army Corps.' On the first two pages he lists, 'from my little notebook', the names of 192 places in France and Belgium 'held, rested in or fought in during my service'. Finally, and with a touch of mystery, he records the ranks above rifleman he held —lance-corporal, corporal and sergeant, 'for various periods, not confirmed'—and his medical category—'CIII, Defective Eyesight, Not to be sent abroad'.

Though the journal gives few dates or exact localities of the many actions described and is of historic interest mainly because of the paucity of first-hand accounts by private soldiers, it is instantly gripping as a human document. It soon emerges that Atkins, because of his eyesight, should never have taken part in the fighting at all. It was through a series of Army blunders that he found himself in the thick of it on the Somme and Ypres fronts. And he was convinced that it was official embarrassment over this that led to his promotions not being confirmed and that deprived him of decorations.

'I was recommended five times for a medal,' he writes. 'The grievance about it all exists in my mind to this day and is a main reason for writing this book.' The grievance was understandable. Justifiably or not, he believed that he should have emerged from the war as a VC.

But the journal is a great deal more than a chip-on-the-shoulder lament. It brings to life the world of the Poor Bloody Infantryman ('You lived like rats, fed like rats and died like rats')—a basically different world from that described by officer writers such as Robert Graves, Siegfried Sassoon, Edmund Blunden. Atkins himself (who was known as Tom) emerges as a very different PBI to the popular conception of a Tommy Atkins. With a questioning mind and an observant eye, he was a bit of a lone wolf, resentful of arbitrary authority, doing things his way. 'I had my own views and could not help being myself,' he writes. 'The Army could not change me.'

The journal begins in 1914 with the closure of the London firm in which Atkins worked as a designer of advertising signs, and his first army medical. He could not read the small letters on the board and was turned down. But, partly because his younger brother Alf had already joined up, he was determined to get into the army and was finally accepted for the Home Service Section. He asked if there was an opening in the Army Pay Corps, was told there was not and was posted to a rifle regiment at Winchester.

The Quartermaster had some difficulty in finding uniform and boots large enough to fit him. Under canvas at Sheerness, he again attracted attention.

'Bayonet fighting was well to the fore in our training and I knew I should never make it my favourite weapon. For the first time I started to think for myself and continued to do so throughout my service. I refused to accept the army principle "You are not here to think but to obey".

'So I must learn defence against the enemy's bayonet and shoot him while we are fencing. This does not please the sergeant, who tries all ways to get at me. "Your defence is good but you don't attack. What's your idea—to keep him trying to reach you until he drops dead from exhaustion?" I said, "No, but to shoot him while I am fencing. I have shot you many times in imagination." "We've still to see if you CAN fire."'

Atkins passed his test on the range, but not without again asserting himself.

'At long distances I could not see the bullseye but managed by imagining a line from the corners cutting the middle and firing at that. I got into trouble for firing too quickly but explained I had to get it over quickly because it was a strain on my eyes. I then asked if I could fire my rifle without putting my shoulder to it. The sergeant explained to the officer my theory of shooting while bayonet fighting. "Well, let him have a go," said the officer. So I fired with the rifle by my side and extended in front. "That's the first time I've seen a rifle used as a revolver." The sergeant said, "He's the fastest man I've seen at loading and firing."

'Why was this? We were told not to touch any part of the rifle except to clean out the barrel, but I got some fine emery paper and, with oil, worked on the bolt until it slid easily. I

87

also oiled all my cartridges in their clips and at odd moments I used to lie in my tent and practice. I also learned to load with ten cartridges and then work an extra one into the firing position. This last was not allowed but I could always do it safely.'

At the end of the course Atkins, who makes no mention of spectacles and could presumably see clearly at shorter distances, paraded in front of the camp doctor.

'In front of me was my pal Jock from Paisley. The doctor said, "What are you down Home Service for?" Jock replied, "I've lost one ear drum and am slightly deaf in the other." The doctor said, "Splendid, you won't be troubled with the bombardments. AI." Then he looked me up and down. "And what is the matter with a great fellow like you?" I said, "Nothing, except the Army won't pass me for overseas on account of my eyesight." He said "Well, if you can't see them, they will damn well soon see you! AI." When I told the sergeant I had passed AI he laughed and said it must be the sea air.'

With a last promise to his recently-wed wife that he would 'not volunteer for any dangerous work but only do my duty', Atkins sailed for France—and more confusion. On parade with his draft at Le Havre, he was watching artillery firing across the valley 'with my eyes screwed up as is my habit when trying to see distant objects', when he was spotted by the inspecting colonel. After interrogating him, the colonel removed him from the draft and ordered him to report sick. The doctor told him he must wait for an optician, and he was left behind by the draft as an 'oddment'.

An impasse seemed to have been reached when the camp sergeant major informed him that he could not draw rations for him because he did not belong to a battalion, and that he would have to return to England. 'I can't do that', Atkins pointed out, 'because they'll ask me what battalion I'm from. But suppose you ask me again what battalion I'm from, and I say one, will that be all right?' As 'the only way out of the situation' the sergeant major agreed and Atkins made a critical tour of the camp, chatting up oddments from a number of battalions who were waiting to go back to the front. He finally opted for the 16th battalion.

When a visiting optician at length tested his eyes, he prescribed glasses and wrote "Must wear glasses" on his pay book. 'Strange as it may seem,' Atkins writes, 'I never took advantage of the fact that, if I broke or lost them, I had only to show my pay book to be sent back to base for replacement. I might also add that I never wore them as they reflected Very lights and, so my pals told me, were like searchlights.'

When he arrived at battalion headquarters, Atkins was told that all non-combatant jobs were filled. 'They must have been relieved when I said "I'll join the battalion with the boys." The sergeant-major said, "Oh well, if that's what you want you'd better go in my old platoon, Number 8. They're the scruffiest, don't-care lot of scroungers in the British Army. Worst on parade—but in the line the pick of the regiment."' So burly, CIII Rifleman Atkins arrived at the front, a bit of a mystery man but soon accepted. 'As I hated parade ground drills and ceremonials, I fitted into this platoon very well. I was always happier up the line.'

Revealingly in the journal, written in retirement, Atkins not infrequently quotes remarks that were made about him, directly or overheard. He recalls his company captain saying on one occasion: 'You're a queer fellow, Tom, I've often heard tales about you. One thing, the men believe in you.' He has the introvert's self-questioning absorption as he looks back over the years, seeing himself out there in the thick of it all, making his tiny mark. And that he did make something of a mark is clear from his first account of the Somme front. After a bitter winter the deep-frozen ground had thawed into a morass of mud.

'Our trench-coats became so heavy that we had to discard them. Even rifles were covered in mud—except mine. My parcels from home were always wrapped in linen from the inside of cocoa tins and I wrapped strips of it, well oiled, round my rifle. So when the inspection came mine was the only one passed. The captain, who did not see my oily rag cover, ordered me to do no sentry or other duties but to go round and see that all rifles were kept like mine.

'As I could move from end to end of the trenches and bring news along, they used to wait for my visits. "What was that big bang at the end, Tom?" and so on. Even after the weather improved and the job was not necessary I continued my visits. As the younger lads started to come out I would be called for to calm them down if any casualties occurred. The best way was to put them to work and pretend to be hard. On one occasion a young lad was crying because his pal had been killed and he'd promised to look after him. What should he tell the boy's mother? "Who said you were going to get home to tell his mother? Someone will be telling your mother if you don't get this trench built up. Come on now, let's get on with it." Often they would work up a bit of resentment against my hard heart and that helped a lot. They didn't know how sorry I was for them. I was now a fixture on this job. I called it Moral Support.'

There is little bitterness in Atkins' attitude to the enemy. 'We looked at them as "old Jerry" across No Man's Land, to be bashed when we had the chance. No real hatred, not even when we were being heavily shelled. It was "I wonder what's upset Jerry tonight?" and often there would be more feeling against our own artillery for not returning the fire.' Atkins even describes occasional collusion between the two sides.

'When a patrol was really necessary we went willingly, but often we were sent out just as a matter of form. The Germans were no doubt sent out in the same way. Both sides knew that if they started to attack each other, the guns might open up from both sides and the patrols could be wiped out. So we often had an agreement. On one occasion a road ran through our lines across No Man's Land and through the German lines. We used to crawl in the ditch on the right of the road and they would crawl on the left. When we got near the middle one would put up a helmet on a rifle and back would come the sign in the same way. We would then sit down and wait. After some time we would again put up the rifle and helmet, or sometimes even stand up and wave, and get the answering sign. And so back to report all quiet. Of course care had to be taken in case another lot had relieved them and might have other views.'

It was on a patrol that Atkins had his first close encounter with the enemy.

'The German trench was about 500 yards in front of us and just below a rise in the ground. For some nights noises could be heard and it was thought the enemy was advancing the trench. We formed up a fighting patrol in daylight so that we could know who would be next to us. The captain put me on the extreme right. On my left was a lance-corporal I didn't know with the Military Medal ribbon. Someone told me he was a daredevil and would go right to the enemy lines. So I supposed I might have to, too.

'At dark we started to crawl out. I kept my eye on the lance-corporal and when he stopped I stopped. Then somehow I lost sight of him. Has he gone forward? I feel sure he has. I work to the left but no one is there. I crawl rapidly forward to make up ground. Still no signs of the rest. I crawl up a shell-hole and look over the top. There are two Germans lying in the next one. I slide back and wait. No whisper or sound. I look again. They are dead. I crawl round this shell-hole and am on a sloping bank. Suddenly I hear a voice. Is it a Scottish accent? I know the Scotties are on our right. Have I crawled in a circle and come back in front of them? I raise my head and am looking right into the German trench.

'I see parties coming out of dugouts with shovels and scoops. I hear them splashing through water and see them scooping

water away. Suddenly I freeze. It has just struck me that if I
can see them they can see my head. I start to slide backwards
and when a little way back turn and wriggle as fast as I can.
After some way I get up, take a few steps and get caught in
barbed wire. While I am untangling myself, a voice comes:
"What are you doing out there, Tom?" It is the patrol back
in the trench.

'The company sergeant-major comes up and I tell him
where I have been. He hurries me to the captain, who is making
out his report in his dugout. I don't know what the others have
told him but he alters his report to say there is eyewitness
evidence that the German trench is water-logged. He roars
with laughter when I describe my patrol and that I had done
it all because I had a Military Medal lance-corporal next to
me. I suspected afterwards that the patrol had never moved
very far.'

Although Atkins plays down the horrors of war, he hints
at the carnage in a description of the divisional burial
party to which he was attached during the third battle of
Ypres. 'We were just behind the battleline, under shellfire
aimed at reinforcements coming up, and sometimes the
padre would say, "We must not sacrifice the living for the
dead", and we would wait till the shellfire eased a little.
We worked hard digging the graves but could hardly keep
up. The service was just a very few words, sometimes over
two or three, sometimes over thirty or forty. Each spot was
given a marker, but who could say how long it would be
there. Identification was not always possible. It made me
realise how very insignificant what is left can be after we have
passed on. And how soon a fighting force can become litter on
a battlefield!'

In describing actions in which he took part he frequently
changes gear into the present tense, as though the memory is
still close. In his sector at the start of the final Allied offensive
in 1918 (by which time he had a dual role as rifleman and certi-

ficated signaller and had been promoted, temporarily, to corporal), a railway cutting was the first objective.

'As we went up the hill Germans kept popping up out of
holes in the ground and putting their hands up. We waved them
back behind us. The enemy machine guns kept up a fire but
our machine gun barrage had now reached the cutting. We
go in with a rush and the Germans flee out as we come in.
One machine-gunner is hiding in a dug-out. When we get
him out the captain is questioning him when he shoots one of
our men with a small revolver hidden in his hand. He does not
last a second.

'Our troops were in the whole length of the railway cutting
and I am on my usual scrounge. I go along to the left and find
a tunnel leading right down nearly to the river where we
started from. It is stacked from end to end with the packs of the
enemy. I look into one or two and find that they are a new lot,
everything is brand new and they have plenty of cigars and small
comforts in them. I know they would have none of these if they
had been in the line long. I found a tiny revolver and put it in
my pocket. I could have made myself rich if I had gone through
them all but I could not waste time here, I must go back.

'The Germans are now attacking us. I notice that the
German fire is not causing casualties but one or two here and
there are being hit. It looks to me like a sniper in some good
position doing the damage and I conclude it is coming from
the left. I went along and carefully had a look. The only place
he can be is on a raised piece of ground covered with bushes.
Watching I see a faint puff of smoke and hear the report and
am now certain that is where he is. I have my usual ten shots
and the extra one loaded. I know he will not fire my way as he
is too near and would give the game away so I get comfortable
and rest my rifle. Another shot comes and I let fly with the
whole eleven into the bushes.

'Nothing happens for a long time so I go along a bit further
and find a gully leading out to the bushes. I stand there looking

down this gully. Have I got him and is it safe to go on? I feel I have got to know. I will never be satisfied unless I find out if I have got him. So I crawl out to the bushes and there he is, telescopic rifle and all, and he has paid the price. He only had a belt on and this I took and came back. I kept it as a razor strop for years.

'The attack by the Germans now became heavy. They drove our men back and I signalled for help with the lamp but the battery ran out. I then used my flags until a bullet cut the sticks of both of them. No answer came. The Germans are now back into the railway cutting both sides of us. A bullet smacked into my pack, though I did not know it at the time. It ruined everything including my leather gauntlet gloves, smashing my mess tin and cutting my spare clothes and scarves to ribbons. The captain said, "We must get out of here but it's going to be a job." This is where my scrounging comes in. I had found the tunnel so was able to lead us all right back to the river in safety, across the tree trunks and into the shelter of a sunken road.'

Atkins was wounded only once in the war. Nine months after arriving at the front he was hit by shrapnel in the shoulder and spent three months convalescing in England, most of the time at Lord Clinton's estate near Torquay, where his truculent attitude to authority quickly antagonised the prim, elderly Matron. It is in a description of a later leave that he indicates the gulf between the trenches and the home front.

'Arriving at Victoria we change our French money and out into Civvy Street. Catching sight of my bus I get on, cluttered with pack and rifle, and sit on a seat for three. The conductor says "Where are you from, mate?" I say: "Just behind Passchendaele." Although I squeeze up in the corner as the bus fills, no one will sit next to me until a workman opposite comes across. "Don't look so hurt, son," he says. "I for one am proud to sit next to you." I said, "I don't suppose you will catch anything, it's too bad even for THEM where we are." It was a queer feeling being on leave, you felt that you did not belong, it was a sort of lost feeling.

'On one occasion I had changed into my civvy clothes and was going to visit my parents. On the tram it is crowded with girls going to munition work. I hear giggling behind me and one says, "Go on, give it to him". A girl sitting behind me touches my shoulder and hands me a white feather. I get up and, taking out my pay book, smack it across her face and say, "Certainly I'll take your feather back to the boys at Passchendaele. I'm in civvies because people think my uniform might be lousy, but if I had it on I wouldn't be half as lousy as you." Most of the girls started to take my part but I said, "Don't bother. There are girls out there driving under fire and they have no time to give feathers."'

One of the often-repeated tales that helped while away the long periods of waiting at the front concerned a soldier who had heard that another man was living with his wife in their home. When he went on leave the Colonel made him promise that he would not harm either of them. 'He had told no one he was coming and when he got there learned from his mother that his wife went out to work,' Atkins writes. 'He broke a window to get into his home and found the wood axe. Then, starting at the top of the house, he smashed and slashed everything—furniture, bed, bedding, tables, curtains, right the way through until he had left nothing whole. He left a note saying "You can have him and all the home." He was quite resigned when he came back. The fun started when we tried to think of something he had missed, but we could not. "I bet you forgot the knives, Jim", but he hadn't, he'd broken the blades. For a long time after, when a man had not received a letter from home for some time, he would say jokingly "Jim, you'd better lend me your axe!"'

Atkins no doubt echoes his front line companions in his derisory attitude to base area ceremonial and regular army spit-and-polish. When conferences were held at the Army

Headquarters bungalow behind Ypres, regiments were required to provide sentries in turn and vigorous complaints were made if they did not correctly salute the different-ranking brass hats. When Atkins was picked he remembered reading in a history of the Kings Royal Rifles that, in a confined space, a sentry could stand with his rifle across his left arm, the only salute being to bring it down and tap it.

'This was a confined space all right, a narrow verandah. I took up my post and up and down I went, giving this salute to all. I got plenty of glares as high-ranking officers arrived and many a look at my cap badge. Our company captain, who had warned me about correct saluting, comes along with our colonel. A look of amazement crosses their faces. Later a staff captain comes out. "What drill is that, sentry?" he asks. I say, "KRR drill for a sentry in a confined space, sir." He goes back in.

'After the conference our captain sent for me. "Tell me, was that drill KRR drill and was it ever official?" I told him about the history and said that, even if I had not read it correctly, no one but a KRR would know if it was right or not. He told me there had been a proper riot at the conference. One general said it was cavalry drill and most of the line regiments said you could expect the Rifles to be different, they always were. Our colonel had said it was correct but told the captain afterwards he hadn't the faintest idea if it had ever been used. I had played on the certainty that no one would like to condemn it and find that they were wrong.'

As a prize example of brass hat buffoonery Atkins recalls an occasion when the battalion was ordered to parade for a general who had an important message.

'All smartened up, we walk several miles from our rest camp to a field, where we stand for two hours wondering what it is all about. Eventually the general arrives, takes up his stand on a raised platform round which we, and hundreds from other regiments, form a square. The General says: "It has come to the notice of the British Army Authority that Britain's oldest Allies are being referred to as the Pork and Beans. I refer to the Portuguese. This must cease forthwith. That is all."

'So now, if anyone did not know it, they will also call them Pork and Beans. In fact as we marched back one of our marching songs was fitted to include, "You all know what it means, If you call them Pork and Beans". And later a song was made beginning:

> The Germans call us Tommy,
> We always call him Fritz,
> We call a Frenchman Froggy,
> Which sends him into fits.
> But our very ancient Allies—
> You know who that means—
> Must NEVER be referred to
> As the good old Pork and Beans.'

Apart from the civilian French, with whom he appears to have got on quite well despite his ignorance of their language, Atkins is apt to regard foreigners with a mixture of amusement and suspicion. Of the Chinese Labour Corps, who were stationed behind the Ypres front, he writes: 'They were a queer lot and most seemed to walk about in their long pants. They never seemed to lace their boots up—perhaps this was because they took them off to run, as they did when the tear-gas shells first came over. At first they sniffed hard and seemed to enjoy the smell, but when their eyes began to water it was boots off and up the road. They were very fond of stripes and would sew them on their arms by the dozen, showing them to us with pride. The French hated them and were afraid of them.'

Of the Portuguese he remarks: 'They sent a few regiments to the front but we did not take them very seriously. In fact when we met a regiment at a station and exchanged cigarettes with them, we noticed that they took theirs out of their gas masks.

On looking inside we found that they had no gas masks in the container. We never knew whether they had not been given the inside part or if they had thrown it away to make room for cigarettes and oddments.'

Predictably he found the Americans, whom he first met in the Ypres area in 1918, too cossetted and cocky by half.

'They were quite inexperienced and there were lots of faults with their equipment. They had silk socks, and this caused sore feet. Their gaiters soon lost their buttons and gaped open—lots of our fellows sold them half of their puttees for twenty francs. Their breeches were too tight at the knees and, although they were smart, their knees were soon through.

'The American sanitary man attached himself to ours. He was hung all round with pouches containing fly killer, disinfectants and chemicals and had a kit of tools. He asked our sanitary man what he had got and he said, "Only this bloody shovel." Another one had a great sword thing hung on him about two feet long and a foot wide at the end. Our boys said: "Jerry will murder you if he sees that—they'll think you are the Headsman! What is it for?" He said, "I'm a machine-gunner and that is to chop branches to camouflage the guns." We said: "Chuck it away—there are no branches left up here."

'A group I was talking to were boasting they had come to finish the war. So what were they stuck in the trenches for when they should be getting at the enemy? I said, "Well, wait until I get out before you start." A little later they tried a large-scale patrol and were nearly all wiped out. I suppose they learned in time.'

Only one precise date is given in the entire journal—13 April 1918, during the last German offensive. This was the day on which he revenged his brother's death and saved the life of a friend—a day that was to haunt him all his life. And it is as though to underline the authenticity of his account that he devotes a whole page to a diagram of the action.

'We have been shifted about and we know something big is on and we shall be in it when they have made up their minds where we are to go. From Caestre we move to Bailleul and then we know whatever it is has started for the place is all knocked about. About 5.30 pm we move up to the forward area. Our colonel comes along as we sit by the road. He is upset, we can see. Following him is the sergeant major. He has a message for us. We are going into the line and must hold on at all costs. Fight to the last and no surrender. No wonder the colonel is unhappy. Soon we get on the move and arrive at the trenches. I cannot remember but believe it was the Staffords or Leicesters we relieved. "Where is Jerry?" we ask and they say, "We don't know, somewhere out there," and wave all round. "There is a very heavy attack expected," they say.

'All day long on the 12th we wait but nothing happens. On the morning of the 13th at daybreak it is misty. Some of our platoon are playing cards and I am wandering up and down in my usual way. I look over the parapet and as I do so a low explosive wire-cutting shell bursts right over my head, missing our men and wounding some others. How I escaped I do not know as I was nearest to it. But I get concussion, my nose and ears bleed and I am peppered with powder dust driven into the skin by the explosion. At the same time I see hundreds of Germans going along in front of the trenches. Not towards us but parallel. I rush down the trench shouting "They are coming over". We soon find they are advancing each side of us and we are end on to them, as will be seen in the diagram.

'A man comes from the forward end and we say "Who are you?" and he says, "I am the only one left of C Company and I think D and A are gone and some of B who are at the top end". The Germans have now advanced past us back and front and we are certain that A, C and D are gone because they were across the advance. The sergeant says, "I'm sorry, Tom, I can't get you away yet." I say, "I'll be all right present-ly." The Germans seem to have stopped advancing and are taking shelter. They are not firing at us, we are now in the middle of them and they are evidently confused. Where the firing is coming from is in the middle and to fire would be to shoot their own men.

'The captain holds a conference and we decide that, as soon as the enemy realise the position, we shall be cut off, if we are not already. So we must retire. As we do so we come to a part where the Worcesters are. We mix with them and I see a mound and climb on top (see diagram).

'Now I had received a letter some days previously to say my brother had been killed. He was serving with the Royal Artillery and had been killed by a long-distance shell twenty miles behind the lines. We were very close. There I am on the ground and crowds of Germans in front of me working their way from left to right of me. Suddenly I think of my brother and I will be revenged. Lying down amongst some bushes on top of the mound I settle my rifle in an easy position and start to shoot them down. This was the only time in the war that was mine and mine alone. At all other times I was part of the war machine and killing was just part of the day's work, with no personal feelings. I had forgotten all about where I was and for all the sentiments I had for them they might have been clay pipes at a shooting gallery.

'I kept firing until my rifle was red hot. Once started on destruction I do not know when I should have finished but a Worcester officer climbed up and, touching my boot, said: "What are you doing, they are the other side." I climbed down and said, "Get up and look, sir, they are this side as well." He soon got down and split the men to fire from both sides.

'Soon it was decided to retire to the village of Neuve Eglise. When we got to the end of the trenches we came to a long open road leading to the village (see diagram). Jack Priestley and I are left behind at the mouth of the trench with orders to keep firing down it until all the others are safe in the village. We kept up a fire but did not see any enemy in the trench and kept looking anxiously at the road. As soon as they had all got into the village we started.

'By now, as will be seen from the diagram (arrows), the Germans had realised the position and turned inwards and were sweeping the road with machine guns. The bullets were kicking up the dust like rain on a pond and we could see them as they swept up and down the road. There was not a stick of shelter along the whole length. We had not gone far when Jack was hit in the leg. I said, "Keep going, Jack, as long as you can." I realised that I was not too good and wondered if I could carry him. Suddenly he stopped. "You'll have to bind my leg up, Tom." I said all right and so we had to stand there in the middle of a hail of bullets while I got out my field bandage and undone it. I did the best thing under the circumstances, I bound his leg up outside his trousers as tightly as I could and said, "Now try, Jack," He hobbled a few steps and then said, "I can go no further." All right, so I must carry him. I throw away my pack off my back. It was a great loss to me as it was a special one and everything in it was lightweight and had been sent out from home. I take him on my back. He is only a short fellow but he must be solid. I struggle along and the bullets still sweep around us. If only I had not had that shell burst I could have managed easily. Somehow I get to the entrance of the village and a machine gun officer runs out and helps us to safety.

'He carried Jack to the aid post and said to me, "All right, old chap, I'll soon get you seen to." I said, "I am all right" and refused to go into the aid post. I told him I must catch up with the boys. He asked me my name and number and regiment and said "I'll get any other particulars from your pal. I'm going to put you in for the highest award any man can get."

It is here that Atkins digresses into a full airing of his 'grievance'. He claims that the rumour got round his company that he was 'in for the VC' and that he later learned that the machine-gun officer had in fact put in his recommendation.

How far his account of this action has been coloured, consciously or unconsciously, to substantiate his belief that he was robbed of glory because he was 'not officially there', can now only be conjecture. So, too, must be the accuracy of his statement that the letter of thanks he learned had been sent to him by Jack Priestley never reached him because it had been 'kept from him'.

'I have often tried but never found Jack, my pal', he writes at the end of the journal. 'Perhaps he imagines me decked with medals. If I had got them they would only be in the drawer with my war medals. Nevertheless the grievance still exists in my mind to this day and is the main reason of this book. There it will remain, locked up in this book.'

For his discharge at the end of the war, Atkins, with a broken ankle, was back where he had started, at the Winchester Depot. And back where he started as plain Rifleman E. A. Atkins, 26699. He records his final interview with a Southern Command colonel.

'Colonel: "Sit down, young man, you are a civilian now. Tell me, how did you break your ankle?"'

'Atkins: "Chasing Germans out of France, sir."'

'Colonel: "What were you doing out there?"'

'Atkins: "I was with my battalion, as I was all through except for three months when wounded on the Somme Front."'

'Colonel (turning to the officer seated next to him): "I told you that this went on."'

'Atkins: 'Excuse me, sir, but I know what you mean. I know what is on those papers."'

'Colonel: "Never mind, young man, you have done your bit and are safe home."'

'Atkins: "Yes, but I tried to be A1 and they would not mark me. But having sent me to the Front without changing my papers, it is unfair."'

'Colonel: "In what way?"'

'Atkins: "Well, sir, I was recommended five times for a

medal and now I know why I was never awarded one. Officially I was not there."

'Colonel: "Never mind, medals are not much use in civil life, are they?" '

Atkins' journal was brought to the notice of *The Sunday Times* by the wife of the auctioneer who had come across it. 'I found it very hard to put down after reading the first page,' she wrote. 'I have often thought about finding out about this man, but wouldn't know where to start.'

The first clue as to Atkins' peacetime identity came from the Imperial War Museum—two letters written by him to the BBC in 1963. They had been among a pile of correspondence from war veterans sent to the Museum by the BBC after they had finished sifting material for their television series on the Great War. Atkins had submitted a copy of his journal, which the producer found 'good'. But he was out of the running when a research assistant phoned him at his home and found him 'very deaf and slow'.

A seven-page letter Atkins wrote after this telephone call, apologising for his deafness and expressing his eagerness to 'co-operate in any way,' touchingly suggests the isolation of the retired war veteran obsessively reliving those incredible years but with no one to share them with. 'I was asked if the facts could be relied on, I say every word is true, my memory as in all old people is better in the past than yesterday,' he writes. 'Besides I was a soldier in every sense. I studied details and loved the life . . . In the field I was happy, I kept a diary, as I mentioned this was dangerous so I kept dates in a separate place (my pocket Testament). This was lost so I am unable to connect . . . You will notice that I have a grievance running through my book, this is personal, I could not take it out of the book. If I have presumed by again writing, I am sorry . . .'

The address on the letters led to a semi-detached house in a quiet surburban road in Gants Hill, Essex. The next-door neighbour, who had known Atkins over a number of years, said he had died there in 1966, his wife two years later. She remembered him as a big, bespectacled man, rather hard of hearing, 'very quiet, kept himself to himself, but very nice'. She gave the address of his closest surviving relative, the widow of his youngest brother who for many years had lived next door.

His sister-in-law and her married daughter could well remember him busily writing the journal after he had retired as partner of a building and decorating business. They had not read it and were surprised that it should have aroused anyone's interest. They could not think how it had ended up in a Wanstead attic.

Atkins' closest friend, now also dead, was a fellow-member of the Ilford Aquatic Club. Freshwater fish and gardening were his hobbies. The room in which he wrote—hearing from far away and long ago the 'monstrous anger of the guns', brooding perhaps on how differently life might have turned out had he been Tommy Atkins, VC—looks out on the trim back garden and the fish-pond for which he had won a number of prizes.

5   *A Lad Goes to War*

It was Sunday morning, 4 August 1914, when Bert Chaney's mother kissed him goodbye and said 'Be a good boy. Have a good time,' and his father, an ex-soldier, looked at him critically and announced, 'You'll never last out the week. You're so thin a couple of long route marches will finish you.'

But the 18-year-old eldest son felt 'proud as Punch' as, with full kit and rifle, he swung down the road from their home and turned at the corner to call back to his waving brothers and sisters: 'Bye-bye, see you next Sunday evening.' He was off to his first annual camp with the 7th London Territorial Battalion at Beachy Head.

That same day Britain declared war on Germany. Chaney was not to get back again into civilian life for 4½ years. The Territorials were mobilised and with the rest of his comrades he signed on for active service overseas, giving his age as the required 19.

Chaney's 55,000-word journal, 'A Lad Goes to War', was written in retirement more than fifty years after the Armistice. 'This will be no history of the war,' he writes in a foreword, 'but simply happenings as they affected me at the time—my thoughts, my observations, my fears and doubts and occasional sorrows.' Here again is the world of the Poor Bloody Infantry, rarely depicted in a first-hand account. As an NCO with the Signallers, Chaney's job was to keep communications flowing rather than to kill Germans. But he saw as much of the action on the Somme and Ypres fronts as many infantrymen armed with rifle and bayonet. And what he saw could not be forgotten.

The journal opens with the buoyancy and keen sense of excitement felt by hundreds of thousands of the first young civilian soldiers. After training he arrived by troopship at Le Havre on 17 March 1915, and next morning his battalion marched through the town to the railway marshalling yard.

'We signallers, each pushing a bicycle loaded with a reel of wire or a telephone, led the line of march, whilst just behind rode the colonel and the adjutant on their fine chargers. Behind them came the Lord Mayor of London's Silver Prize Band, playing our regimental march, "My Lady Greensleeves", then the companies of infantrymen, the transport bringing up the rear. Buttons, badges and boots highly polished, we swaggered down the hill, everyone in perfect step. We'd show these Frenchmen what a London Terrier Regiment was like. Now we had arrived in France the war was as good as over, so we thought.'

Their first slight shock came when they halted beside the train and found that, except for one carriage marked 'Officers Only', the remainder of the train consisted of closed railway waggons, each marked on the side in large letters: '8 Chevaux ou 40 Hommes'. During the two-day journey the horses took precedence over the men ('Horses were expensive and needed taking care of whereas a Tommy could be got for only a shilling a day'). But at Bethune, where they were billeted in a disused factory, their spirits rose.

For a youth who had never been abroad, let alone to a war, everything was novel and exciting—the language, the French people, the shops and cafes, the little carts pulled by dogs over the cobblestones, the constant coming and going of troops—the French still wearing pre-war uniforms of dark blue with red facings, the Zouaves with baggy cotton trousers tucked into their boots, short fancy jackets and pill-box hats. In their barracks even their lavatories were to be marvelled at—'a hole in the ground, on each side a short rail attached to the partition walls at an angle for easy grasping'.

For Chaney there was a particular eye-opener one day when he noticed a long queue of soldiers quietly standing two by two being kept in order by a couple of military policemen.

'Thinking there might be a concert or cinema—we called them living pictures at that time—I asked what was going on. "A bit of grumble and grunt," I was told. "Only costs two francs." Puzzled, I asked what that meant. "Cor blimey, lad. Didn't you learn anything at all where you come from?" They thought me a proper mug. Fancy a lad like me, and a Cockney at that, not knowing what that meant—and didn't I know what a red lamp stood for? These places, I was told, were not for young lads like me, but for married men who were missing their wives.

'One day I looked inside and saw a large room with a long bar down one side, the room crowded with men, with the girls standing on the stairs leaning over the bannister, presumably waiting for the next customer. They all wore voluminous dressing-gowns and anything less likely to excite a man would be hard to imagine. A leg might be showing, or even a bare shoulder, to give the impression they had nothing on underneath. To my young eyes they all looked like disapproving mothers watching with distaste the antics of their young offspring below.'

Throughout their stay in Bethune could be heard the distant sound of shells and machine-gun fire, reminding them that they were not far from the firing line. It was with mounting excitement that they finally approached the trenches.

'There was so much of interest as we moved forward, especially the wonderful display of starlights and Verey lights, fired into the air to light up No Man's Land. As the line stretched for miles and miles both to left and right, it gave one the impression of standing in a semi-circle of lights, somewhat similar to a firework display at the Crystal Palace.

'We marched for some time in column of fours as a battalion, until we were met by some Scots soldiers who were to act as our guides. From then on we went forward in single file. We had been marching easy until then, singing and smoking, but their first order was "No smoking and no talking." They explained that the light from a cigarette could be seen for miles and, as any noise at night carried a long way, there was no need to advertise the fact we were on our way.

'As we came to our respective positions in the front line there was a constant crackle of machine gun and rifle fire and a continual buzzing went on around us, mostly over our heads. Someone was foolish enough to ask our guide for an explanation of the buzzing sounds. Muttering "Bloody Rookies" to himself he explained they were German bullets flying by and intended for any fool who cared to stand upright. Almost immediately we arrived at the front line breastworks, one of the lads stood up and looked over the top. "Get down, you bloody fool!" yelled the guide, but the bloody fool simply turned his head to ask, "Is that where the Germans are?" There was no time to answer him for almost at once he fell in a heap in front of us.

' "Stretcher-bearer," shouted the guide without hesitation, while I bent down to ask the lad what had happened. "Something knocked me over. I think I've been hit in the jaw," he answered, and as he spoke spat out a bullet. It had gone through his cheek, busted a couple of teeth and stopped inside his mouth. The guide said he could consider himself bloody lucky, it must have been a spent bullet. "Keep it as a war souvenir," he said, while we all crowded round to inspect the wound and were rather surprised to see what little damage had been done. Nothing to it, we thought.'

The euphoria persisted until the newcomers experienced their first real baptism of fire on the Neuve Chapelle front. For Chaney the moment of truth came when he was out alone during an attack laying a line forward from the support trench.

'As I moved forward, allowing the wire to run from the reel of its own accord, a lad coming back from the line stopped me, saying "Help me, I'm wounded". Hardly taking the trouble to look at him I said I was too busy on my own job and he had better walk back to the dressing station where they could see to him properly. I began to move forward again but he clutched at me, almost crying. "Help me, stop it bleeding." Then I saw his arm muscle was badly lacerated, some of the flesh hanging loose, and the blood flowing fast. He hung on to my arm, looking and sounding so piteous that I decided to stop and help him. He was no older than myself and was possibly afraid he might bleed to death.

'I took the field dressing from its packet, tore off the remnants of his coat sleeve and broke the phial of iodine over the wound. Then I laid the lint on top of the raw part and bandaged round and round his upper arm until all the bandage was used. With a quiet "Thank you" he went on his way to the dressing station. I wondered for a moment or two if I had done the right thing, and then forgot all about him as I picked up my reel of wire and carried on with the job.

'The shelling was now very heavy indeed, the earth seemed to be erupting all around me as I moved forward. And then, on rounding a traverse in the breastworks, I was surprised to see something crouching as if ready to spring—a German, complete with spiked helmet, staring at me. I felt my heart leap into my mouth. All I carried with me was a field telephone and a reel of wire, but I had little time for thought for at almost the same moment that I perceived him I heard the roar and thunder of a salvo of Jack Johnsons, the heaviest of shells, coming very close indeed. I dropped flat to the ground, automatically putting my hands over my head as one of the shells landed right beside me. It rocked the ground under me as it exploded in black smoke, throwing up a volcano of earth and metal. As I lay prone, my body pressed as close as possible to the ground, my mind was racing. What to do about the German in front of me? Was he a prisoner without escort or might he attack me immediately the stuff stopped falling on us?

'After a few seconds of dazed surprise to find myself still alive, I rose to my knees, looking up warily. There was the German in exactly the same position as previously, still staring, and as he did not move I realised with a start he must be dead. By now I was feeling very shaken indeed, but picked up the reel of wire with the intention of continuing my job. Then I heard someone say, "Don't go out there again, lad, you'll never live through it". I am sure he was right and I must admit that by this time I was only looking for an excuse to abandon my job and run for cover. The chap talked to me for a few minutes as we crouched in the shelter of the sandbags. He must have guessed it was my first battle and was doing his best to steady me.

'Returning to headquarters I reported to the sergeant saying I would finish the job as soon as things quietened down a little —or at least that is what I thought I said. He told me afterwards that I burst into the cellar being used as headquarters and babbled of broken wires, Jack Johnsons and dead, staring Germans. He decided that I had the "wind up" and told me to lie down and have a good sleep and I would be all right in the morning. He had the right idea on how to handle a lad, still only 18 years old, and just about ready to crack. Next morning he sent me out again to finish the job but this time another signaller came with me, both to help lay the wire and keep me company. The sergeant knew the comfort of having someone beside you when things are getting too hot, and the return there would be of my own self-confidence. But from then on I maintained a healthy respect for gunfire. The officer who had been in command of our section since before the war, and whom we thought the world of, was killed in this action by a flying piece of shrapnel which tore off his testicles so that he died in a few minutes in terrible agony.'

During the summer of 1915 it was relatively quiet and for part of the time Chaney's battalion made itself at home in an unscathed village just behind the front line.

'Maroc was a pretty mining village of brick terraced houses, with nice gardens front and rear and water pumps standing at intervals along the street. All the mining community had been evacuated and they must have gone in a hell of a hurry as they had left all their belongings behind. When not on duty in the line we were supposed to live in the cellars of the houses and not move about outside in daylight with the risk of drawing enemy fire. But by dodging behind houses and crouching down where necessary, we managed to get all around the village at any time.

'The cherries were ripe in the gardens for picking and a tin of condensed milk and some packets of custard powder we had found in an empty corner shop gave us a sweet that would have been acceptable on any table. There were also fresh vegetables in some of the gardens. Having been deprived of the niceties of life for some time, we tended to spread ourselves and show off a bit. Finding white linen tablecloths we sat at table as if at home. We undressed and went to bed as if we were at home, using any of the underclothes we found in the various chests of drawers. When one of the lads got wounded, he refused to go to the dressing station and it took us some time to discover the reason. He had thrown away his lousy long woollen underpants and was wearing a pair of lady's long white calico bloomers. This would not have been so bad, but they were heavily trimmed with lace and he was imagining the hoots of derision he would receive—and did receive—from the stretcher bearers when they took his clothes off to attend to the wound, which happened to be in his backside.

'Not to be outdone in the manner of keeping house, one bright lad whitened his doorstep, which was the fashion of those days, and polished the brass door knocker and handle till they shone like gold. It was not long before all the houses facing away from the front line received similar treatment. We were all getting very house-proud. Unfortunately for us the Army decided that it was time to make an attack all along this portion of the front.'

This was the battle of Loos, 25-27 September, in which seven British divisions were engaged in a mass assault across a strongly defended wilderness of coalfields, slag heaps and miners' cottages. Following a German counter-attack nothing was gained strategically and there were nearly 50,000 British casualties as against 20,000 German.

During the night of 25 September, Chaney's section was engaged in laying lines half-way across No Man's Land and connecting up field telephones to them.

'The principle was that our signallers, moving forward with each wave of the infantrymen, would pick up the phones as they reached them and let headquarters know how each wave was progressing. On the whole this worked out rather well and, although there were inevitably a number of casualties, enough signallers were left to keep moving forward with the infantry companies as they reached their objectives. It was essential to keep communications open at any cost in order to give warning of impending counter-attacks, when our guns could concentrate fire where necessary.'

Chaney witnessed the attack from advanced headquarters in the front line to which he was attached.

'Someone took a football over the top with him and it was kicked from one to the other across No Man's Land until forgotten in the final bayonet charge through the enemy barbed wire. This was not cut up by the preliminary bombardment as much as expected and there were a lot of casualties as the men scrambled to get through it. The slag heap on our right flank—about 100 feet high and 100 yards long, all loose shale—gave a lot of trouble, but the company detailed to capture it gradually forced their way up the sides, throwing grenades as they went, and although our casualties were very heavy they pushed the Germans back until, reaching the top, the position was reversed and they could throw their grenades down among the retreating Germans.

'On our left the new Scottish 15th Division went forward full of fire and fight. Their objective was Hill 70 and they went so fast that before they knew what had happened they found themselves in the town of Lens, miles in front of anyone else and more or less marooned. There they stayed for some time, all cock-a-hoop, not a German to be seen, until, for some unknown reason, their commanding officer decided to retire. The Pioneers had been brought up and were getting themselves some tea when a troop of Uhlans, German mounted lancers, arrived and attacked. The Pioneers had only picks and shovels to defend themselves with but we heard they put up a grand fight. How we should have liked to have seen it—cavalry with lances against picks and shovels! Instead of holding Hill 70 the Scots retired right through our lines to the rear. This created a bit of a vacuum on our left flank and our colonel wanted to arrest one of the Scots colonels for dereliction of duty or some such thing, while our lads did not improve the situation by telling the Scotties what they thought of them. Of course, it was no fault of the rank and file, they were only carrying out orders.

'Next day, as a result of this boob, the Guards Brigade had to make a special daylight attack to recapture Hill 70. And what an attack. These boys, the remnants of the original Guards, showed us how it should be done, according to army discipline. One got the impression they knew all eyes were on them, moving forward all the time as if on parade. We had a grandstand view of it all. Every German gun that could be brought to bear concentrated on them as they moved forward, leaving us free to stand up in our trenches and watch everything that occurred.

'From about two miles behind our lines they began to advance in column of blobs, that is to say each platoon of about forty men marched tight up to each other to form a diamond shape, each diamond being about fifty yards from the next. As soon as they were spotted the German guns plastered them unmercifully, and occasionally a blob of men would disappear in a cloud of smoke and fire, until suddenly they began to extend in line to left and right, each line some distance from the next. All the time they maintained their forward movement, the men extending to left and right to fill up the gaps as their comrades fell. Then a halt, lying down to fix bayonets. By this time they were at the foot of Hill 70 and their casualties had been enormous. Rising to their feet and again advancing, they disappeared from our view as they made their final charge up and over the hill. They took Hill 70 and later we held it for them to allow them to be relieved that night, completely exhausted men.'

After the battle Chaney's battalion returned to the village of Maroc. 'We found it had been turned into a heap of rubble with trenches running down the streets and even through the remains of houses. Some of us felt like weeping to see it so badly battered, remembering the nice times we had spent there during the summer.'

After a week's home leave ('feeling a bit battered from the Loos stunt') Chaney spent the winter in and out of the line in various sectors. During the Arras offensive in April 1916 he spent two perilous days and nights on Vimy Ridge—'an experience I felt must have taken twenty years off my life expectancy'. They were under constant shellfire (including tear gas shells) and had next to nothing to eat or drink. 'When relieved we almost crawled out on our hands and knees, eyes and nose running from the tear gas that had got into our stomachs, head and ears still ringing from the sound of gunfire. Back at Reserve Headquarters we were quickly refitted and brought up to fighting strength again with new drafts from England, and then, by gradual stages and short marches, we reached the Somme.'

On 15 September, the division took part in the third attempt, since the launching of the Somme offensive on 1 July, to break through the German defences. It was a day that was to foreshadow land warfare of the future—the day the tank first went into action. A closely-guarded British secret, thirty-six Mark 1 tanks spearheaded the attack. And although only eleven of them succeeded in crossing the German front line (the remainder breaking down, being ditched or shot up), the sight of these monstrous-looking machines crawling ahead of the waves of infantry had an immediate shock effect on the enemy. Chaney had a close-up view of the historic occasion. His first incredulous sight of the tanks was three days before the battle.

'We heard strange throbbing noises, and lumbering slowly towards us came three huge mechanical monsters such as we had never seen before. My first impression was that they looked ready to topple on their noses, but their tails and the two little wheels at the back held them down and kept them level. Big metal things they were, with two sets of caterpillar wheels that went right round the body. There was a bulge on each side with a door in the bulging part, and machine guns on swivels poked out from either side. The engine, a petrol engine of massive proportions, occupied practically all the inside space. Mounted behind each door was a motor-cycle type of saddle seat and there was just about enough room left for the belts of ammunition and the drivers.'

On Chaney's sector of the front the debut of the three tanks assigned to them was marked by what might have been a calamitous misjudgement due to inadequate briefing of the tank crews.

'During the night a new trench was dug some fifty yards behind the existing front line as an assembly trench for the attacking troops. The tank crews' maps showed so many trenches to cross before reaching the enemy front line, all to be counted as they went forward. Nobody had thought it

115

worth while to mention that there would be an extra trench dug during the night.

'I was attached to battalion headquarters and the colonel, adjutant, sergeant-major and myself with four signallers had come up to the front line. From this position the colonel could see his men leave the assembly trench, move forward with the tanks, jump over us and advance to the enemy trenches. As a new style of attack he thought it would be one of the highlights of the war.

'While it was still dark we heard the steady drone of heavy engines and by the time the sun had risen the tanks were approaching our front line, dead on time. The Germans must have heard them too and, although they had no idea what to expect, they promptly laid down a heavy curtain of fire on our front line. This had the effect of making us keep our heads down, but every now and again we felt compelled to pop up and look back to see how the tanks were progressing. It was most heartening to watch their advance, we were almost ready to cheer. But there was a surprise in store for us.

'Instead of going on to the German lines the three tanks assigned to us straddled our front line, stopped and then opened up a murderous machine gun fire, enfilading us left and right. There they sat, squat monstrous things, noses stuck up in the air, crushing the sides of our trench out of shape with their machine guns swivelling around and firing like mad.

'Everyone dived for cover, except the colonel. He jumped on top of the parapet, shouting at the top of his voice, "Runner, runner, go tell those tanks to stop firing at once. At once, I say." By now the enemy fire had risen to a crescendo but, giving no thought to his personal safety as he saw the tanks firing on his own men, he ran forward and furiously rained blows with his cane on the side of one of the tanks in an endeavour to attract their attention.

'Although, what with the sounds of the engines and the firing in such an enclosed space, no one in the tank could hear him, they finally realised they were on the wrong trench and moved on, frightening the Jerries out of their wits and making them scuttle like frightened rabbits. One of the tanks got caught up on a tree stump and never reached their front line and a second had its rear steering wheels shot off and could not guide itself. The crew thought it more prudent to stop, so they told us afterwards, rather than to keep going as they felt they might go out of control and run on until they reached Berlin. The third tank went on and ran through Flers, flattening everything they thought should be flattened, pushing down walls and thoroughly enjoying themselves, our lads coming up behind them, taking over the village, or what was left of it, and digging in on the line prescribed for them before the attack. This was one of the rare occasions when they had passed through the enemy fire and they were enjoying themselves chasing and rounding up the Jerries, collecting thousands of prisoners and sending them back to our lines escorted only by Pioneers armed with shovels.

'The four men in the tank that had got itself hung up dismounted, all in the heat of the battle, stretching themselves, scratching their heads, then slowly and deliberately walked round their vehicle inspecting it from every angle and appeared to hold a conference among themselves. After standing around for a few minutes, looking somewhat lost, they calmly took out from the inside of the tank a primus stove and, using the side of the tank as a cover from enemy fire, sat down on the ground and made themselves some tea. The battle was over as far as they were concerned.'

Following this action, the Colonel held a special battalion parade.

'He told us how proud he was of us in the way we had carried out our part in the big push. And he told us that now he had to leave us because he had been ordered to return to England on medical grounds—nothing else would take him away from us, he said. We who had been with him since the beginning had become very fond of the old man and his parting words were remembered and used as a catchphrase on many an occasion afterwards. "Goodbye, lads," he said. "I've got to leave you. The doctors have got me." "The doctors have got me"—only he could have put it that way.

'He was one of those trained in the big public schools and the Royal Military College at Camberley in those far-off days before the war, men who thought they were indestructible, untouchable—and, by God, the way some of them acted, we sometimes thought so too. Marvellous men they were, men one could follow. Sometimes one thought they did not possess a scrap of human kindness, but when it came to the pinch, especially if the honour of the regiment was at stake, they would go through hell and high water to help their own men.'

Chaney describes in some detail the part played by the signallers in the major actions he was engaged in. He had no very high opinion of the various technical innovations passed on to them, culminating in the first primitive type of wireless set. 'Once again the Army showed its marvellous ingenuity for thinking up something damned silly,' he writes about one unwieldy machine, the 'Fullerphone', which was designed to stop the enemy from picking up messages. One of the oddest experiments in communication his section tried out was during an attack in October 1916, on the Butte de Warlincourt, a Gallic burial mound some sixty feet high that dominated the Somme battlefield.

'Instead of relying on our signallers and their lines, an aeroplane would fly overhead during the action and report exactly what was happening on the ground. The observer, sitting in front of the pilot, had an Aldis lamp for sending signals to me, leaning over the side of the fuselage and pointing it at me. This lamp had a pistol-type handle with a trigger for transmitting by Morse Code, the lamp flashing on and off.

'For answering him I had a contraption similar to a giant Venetian blind, yards long and yards wide, pegged out on to the ground to keep it flat and stop it from moving. The slats were painted white on one side and red on the other, with two lengths of rope connecting them all together. By standing at one end and pulling on the ropes it was possible to open the slats to show either red or white, and by using the Morse Code with long or short pulls the plane and I managed to keep up a conversation. We had a few practice trials the day before the attack and great things were expected from this first direct contact with a plane in flight.

'I found a flat space just behind the reserve trenches and close to battalion headquarters on which to peg out my flapper. The thrown up earth from the trench acted as a screen from enemy eyes. We synchronised our watches and waited for the moment of attack. At dawn some 600 men climbed out of their trenches and moved forward at walking pace. If everything went according to plan they would have reached their objective in about a quarter of an hour. Following a scientific bombardment of the Butte, the high-ups anticipated no real opposition.

'The little aeroplane swept over us a minute or two later, flew on to the Butte and then returned to ask "Cannot see them —have they started yet?" Cursing the observer for being such a bloody fool, we told him they had been gone some five minutes and he had better shake himself up a bit or they would have arrived before he could tell us anything at all. The little plane— a thing of bits of wood, string and wire, with scraps of canvas— turned back and swept low, at times almost touching the ground with its wing as it turned this way and that, covering all the ground almost up to the Butte itself. Back he came, the observer hanging over the side pointing his lamp at me like a revolver, with his finger on the trigger spelling out the letters. We were so close to each other I could have heard him if he had shouted were it not for the noise of the engine. Round and round I pivoted to keep him in front of me as I spelt out his message, a signaller beside me writing down on a pad. Then tugging on the ropes, slowly spelling out the Morse symbols on the heavy flaps. Asking, answering. Runners had been dashing backwards and forwards to headquarters with the messages when the adjutant himself came out to stand beside me in the chalky dust, not knowing what to make of it all. The observer's final message was: "Not a thing to be seen. They have disappeared."

'By now this lack of information was worrying everyone at headquarters and I was wishing I had sent some of my lads over with the attacking troops as usual. Then a couple of wounded men crawled back with the information that the battalion had run into very heavy machine gun fire and they thought they were the only ones left. Runners were sent forward to try to contact the battalion. They returned to say it was almost impossible to move out there without drawing machine gun fire on themselves. Later another wounded man crawled back with news that a wounded officer and a few men were still alive, pinned down in a shell hole not half way across No Man's Land.

'That night a runner got to them with orders to retire, and the next night, with the artillery opening up on to the Butte, they managed to creep back. Of the 600 men who had gone over, only one young officer and 49 men, most of them wounded, got back. Later a few wounded who had been lying out in the open also returned. Apparently there had been a lot of well-camouflaged trenches on the Butte untouched by our guns. The Germans had waited until our lads were well out into the open and then, throwing off their covers, opened up a murderous cross-fire. The few survivors had been so pinned down in shell-holes that they were unable to inform us of their plight. Everyone at headquarters was staggered at the enormity and speed of the whole thing—nearly a whole battalion wiped out in less than five minutes.'

The battle of the Somme, the most terrible in British history, in which nearly half a million of the 'flower of the British Empire' were killed or wounded, marked a turning-point for most of its survivors in their attitude to the war. 'To our minds the generals would keep us out here until we were all killed, and although nobody thought of disobeying orders some of the originals continually grumbled at the way the war was going,' writes Chaney. 'We were proud of all the new guns, the new men coming out were just as enthusiastic as we had been originally, but after two years away from home we were beginning to think the war would never end. From now on the veterans, myself included, decided to do no more than was really necessary, following orders but if possible keeping out of harm's way. I have a feeling that many of the officers felt the same way.'

Keeping from freezing was a major front line preoccupation during the ensuing bitter winter. Chaney recalls an occasion when it brought opposing trenches into a kind of brotherhood of mutual suffering.

'One night snow fell making life for the boys in the slit trenches almost intolerable. It was too cold to even hold a rifle, and soon heads could be seen popping up over the top of the German trenches as they stamped about and swung their arms in an effort to keep warm. Our lads followed suit, and before long the war on that part of the front was forgotten in the general endeavour to keep from freezing. Fires were lit in the trenches and men walked about on top without fear of being fired on. This lasted for some days until the brigadier got to hear about it and came round on a tour of inspection. He said he was appalled at what he saw and ordered us to "make a bloody war of it". So firing broke out again and things went back to normal.'

But it was the mud-churned holocaust of Passchendaele, during the third battle of Ypres in the autumn of 1917, that most forcibly impressed on Chaney the seeming indifference to suffering of the 'high-ups'. He watched an attack by men of his division over ground so pitted and churned up by bombardments as to be impassable.

'Over the top they went, out of the mud in the trench into the mud on top. They managed to struggle about halfway across No Man's Land, dragging one foot after the other until getting literally stuck in the mud, unable to move one way or the other. As they wallowed in the mud they were simply so much target practice for the Jerries. They were not even moving targets and the wounded as they fell just quietly drowned in the water-filled shellholes.

'What a slaughter—and what a disgrace to the thinking of our General Staff. Field-Marshal Haig might ride around on his big white horse, accompanied always by his two mounted orderlies, one proudly carrying the marshal's pennant, but his knowledge of conditions up front must have been practically nil. Either that or he and his staff did not give a damn how many men went west in their endeavour to gain a few yards of worthless, useless ground. It looked well in the papers, a report that our troops had advanced. They seldom said how many yards for how many men.'

It was when they were marching back to rest billets from this engagement that Chaney had an unexpected meeting with his father, who was serving as a staff sergeant in charge of an advance field hospital.

'I saw him standing by the roadside anxiously scanning the faces as we passed by, but I had to shout to him and wave my hand frantically before he spotted me. He scrambled through the marching ranks to get to me and gazed at me in astonishment. "My God, son," he exclaimed, "I would never have recognised you. How the hell did you manage to get out of that lot in one piece?" He said that not counting the mud that hid me we all looked more or less the same, grey-looking, unshaven, with staring eyes. He did not believe it could be me. After cleaning up I went to his hospital where he showed me off to his mates and then gave me a right royal feed in the sergeants' mess.'

Chaney devotes relatively little space to rest periods away from the front line. In the dead land behind the Somme front there was nothing to do at night but play cards and

gamble with dice until a divisional concert party was in-
augurated in a Nissen hut. 'We knew all the songs and bawled
them out with gusto, knew the comedian's jokes better than
he did and helped out with dialogue at the slightest provoca-
tion. We loved the manner in which the female impersonators
primped around the stage, doing a Mae West before Mae
West was even thought of, singing soprano, showing off their
figures, wiggling their hips, poking out from a slit skirt—how
daring!—a shapely silk-stockinged leg with maybe a fancy
diamante garter fastened above the knee. We would whistle
and stomp our feet at them, showing our encouragement in no
uncertain manner.'

In between drills and parades there were football and
cricket matches, band concerts, swimming galas if there was a
canal handy, gymkhanas with displays by the gunners and
officers' races. But it was feminine company that most hankered
for.

'After a pay parade we younger lads would dash off to a
farmhouse, if there was one near enough, to eat fried eggs and
beautiful crusty bread, all for a few coppers, while the elder
men usually repaired to the nearest estaminet and sat drinking
the weak French beer, grumbling all the time that it was
nothing like as good as English beer. Some of the girls of the
village would come in to fraternise and enjoy the sing-song
that usually accompanied the drinking. They would stand to
one side in a little group, having quiet little giggles among
themselves about one or other of the men, reckoning they
were quite safe as none of the men understood a word of what
they were saying. I had learned French at school and on
occasion when I went to an estaminet would hear something
that made me blush.

'As one walked along the village street one was always
pestered by small boys asking for chocolate, ragged little
fellows with no shoes or socks, or other boys touting for business
for their elder sisters, shouting as one passed, "Gig-a-gig, my

sister very good. Gig-a-gig, two francs." Some of these boys would accompany these shouts with movements indicative of their sister's business. We'd laugh and walk on, but some of the older men might give them a clip round the ear with a growled "Hop it", and mutter: "These Froggies have no decency at all—it's a disgrace teaching these kiddies to talk that way."

'As more and more Frenchmen were called up, girls took over their jobs. In one small town the barber's daughter took over the job of shaving. There were so many customers that some of the men waited hours for a shave. She was big and buxom, with large, round, slightly hanging bosoms, wearing a blouse of rather thin material with a "V" neckline. The chair for the customer was an ordinary bentwood chair, which meant he had nowhere to rest his head while being shaved. After a small boy had lathered the customer's face, the girl would take up her old-style cut-throat razor and, resting the man's head on her ample breasts, proceed to shave him, turning his head this way and that, leaning over him and pressing his head into her bosom, especially for the upstrokes of the razor around the throat. All the time father was quietly cutting hair at another chair, a proper barber's chair, and just as quietly taking the money and putting it in his pocket.'

Most of the cold, wet winter of 1917 Chaney spent in the Ypres salient. In February 1918 the division moved south to St Quentin on the Somme, where they learned that there were signs of the Germans building up strength for a big attack. They were positioned as the last English troops on the right of the expected attack, linking up with the French and separated by the river Somme from the rest of the British Fifth Army to the north. Chaney made thorough preparations to ensure that his section would maintain communications with battalion headquarters when the Germans struck.

'We had a nice deep dugout in the front line trench on a high bank overlooking the river and with a clear view in all directions. Our first job was to lay extra lines to give us a better chance of keeping communications going in the event of heavy shellfire. By compass I then plotted a small mound of earth some miles behind the front line and set up a signal station there, which was also in contact with headquarters. Now, even if the lines were smashed, I had a visual station to keep headquarters in touch with our front line. We tried test messages with flags and also set up an Aldis lamp for night signals, though if necessary this could be used in daylight too. We set up a heliograph as well, an instrument using the sun's rays reflected on to a mirror back to a distant spot, using Morse Code to break up the rays. A large buzzer acting as an earth wireless was also installed, but as we could only send on it and not receive we would have no idea if our signals were being picked up or not. To cap everything the Royal Engineers sent us two large dogs and four homing pigeons. All in all we were a most complete and formidable signal station, ready for any emergency.

'In the dawn of March 21st it was seen that the whole of our front was blanketed in a thick mist, thickest along and beside the river. One could not see more than a few yards and there was not a breath of wind to dispel it. Then suddenly all hell was let loose. The Germans began such a blanket bombardment that one got the impression that nothing could exist in it and we thanked our lucky stars for our nice deep dugout. The company commander immediately got in touch with headquarters and it was only too apparent that Jerry was launching a real full-scale attack. But not on our front, nor on our side of the river.

'It was hours afterwards that we discovered that he was by-passing us by going down the river on rafts, thereby cutting us off from the rest of our troops on the northern side of the river. We did not figure in the actual attack at all, although Jerry made sure we stayed put by laying down an intense barrage on our front right along the river's edge. As was to be expected in such a blitz, one by one our telephone wires were smashed. We endeavoured a number of times to repair them, going out into the barrage, creeping down communication trenches trying to find the ends of the wires. But in that mist and in that barrage it was a hopeless task and we had to get back to our dugout, thankful still to be in one piece.

'It was impossible to see anything of our visual communication station on the mound, the Aldis lamps were unable to penetrate the mist, even the telescope did not help. Dashing down into the dugout I scribbled two similar coded messages on the special thin paper provided, screwed them up and pushed them into the little containers which clip on to the pigeons' legs. I and one of my boys, each carrying a pigeon, crept up the steps, pushed the gas blanket to one side and threw our birds into the air. Away they flew. We watched them as they circled round a couple of times and, then, like divers, they swooped straight down and settled on top of the dugout. We retrieved them and tried once more but those birds refused to fly in that mist. They had been trained to fly direct to their loft and would not start until they could see it.

'So down into the dugout again to write another message and put it into the small pouch attached to the dog's collar. Leading it to the entrance I gave it a parting slap on the rump, at the same time shouting firmly "Home boy! Allez!" I watched it for a minute or two as it trotted off, then dropped the gas blanket back in position. Even while we were still sighing with relief a wet nose pushed the blanket aside and in crawled the dog, scared out of its wits. All our efforts could not budge him. We pushed and shoved him, pulled him by the collar to get him moving, but he just lay down, clamped his body firmly to the ground and pretended to be asleep. We eventually took the message from his collar, put it on the other dog and tried to send that one on his way. Whether he was more timid than the first dog, or sensed its fear, he would not even move. He dropped flat on his stomach and there was no shifting him. Once again we went through the pushing and pulling, but it was no good.

'So ended all our wonderful preparations for keeping communications going during the attack. Within a few minutes of its commencement we had become completely isolated. The only thing left was that new-fangled wireless buzzer. I put a man on the keyboard who sent out the same message for hours, with no means of knowing if they were receiving us at the other end. As a matter of fact it was all a waste of time. The RE signallers at the other end had already been over-run and killed or captured.'

For six uneasy days the troops south of the Somme remained isolated from the bitter fighting to the north where the Germans, aided by the persisting morning mist, quickly regained the ground they had lost during the British offensive of 1916.

'We were left bewildered but untouched, the Germans not even troubling to shell us after their initial advance across the river. Our communications to battalion headquarters were reestablished, but the RE signals had completely lost touch with brigade and divisional headquarters. We no longer needed the dogs and I sent them back with a coded message just to get rid of them. They were now only too pleased to go, being cooped up in a dugout was not their idea of a good life. I wondered if they ever found their kennels, which I am sure were by then in the hands of the enemy. The pigeons were also released, though they had to run the gauntlet of some trigger-happy Jerries as they flew off, doing one complete circle to get their bearings before flying away west, as straight as a die.'

On the sixth night there were orders to evacuate the position and retire.

'As we fell back through the hitherto untouched countryside, French civilians hurled insults at us and even spat at us. At last the line began to hold, mainly due on our part of the front to Major Carey, an unknown behind-the-line town major. As our boys, dazed and falling asleep as they marched, stumbled along the road he stopped and collected every man he could see, every cook, batman, driver, messman, artilleryman, unmounted cavalryman, any of the odds and sods who, though wearing a uniform, had never used a rifle in their lives. They were given rifles and ammunition taken from the wounded as they passed through our lines, and while we waited we gave them rifle shooting lessons.

'The major, who had the appearance of an old turkey cock as he strode up and down, told us to wait until we could clearly see the enemy. "Then shoot like hell and keep on shooting until you have no more ammo left. Get them before they can get you." This was his order to the motley crew and shoot we did. Maybe the Germans had extended their lines of communication too much or had lost heart to carry on, but it is a fact that this rabble of odds and ends stopped them in their tracks. They must have thought they were up against a new strong reserve force and were halted long enough to allow the generals to collect their scattered thoughts and the remnants of the 5th Army and throw them in to fill in any gaps in the line.

'I was one of those unfortunates who stumbled into this shambles and found everyone lying on the sloping sides of the ditches, resting on the top, all pointing the same way. It was surprising how many there were who had never handled a rifle, but we hoped for the best. We each made little piles beside us of the clips of cartridges for easy reloading, loading with nine cartridges in the magazine and one in the breech, and waited. Nothing seemed to be happening so I thankfully dropped down into the ditch half full of water and fell asleep.

'I was awakened with the shout of "Here they come!" A long way off could be seen an uneven line of men in grey uniforms, almost shoulder to shoulder, moving slowly but steadily forward towards us. Suddenly everyone seemed to be firing and I added my quota to the din. At the beginning of the war I had been a first class shot, but this day I found myself unable to really hold my rifle steady. I found myself jerking the trigger instead of squeezing it, and blinked my eyes every time I fired a shot. Jerk, fire, blink—so it went on, for hours as it seemed. God knows where my shots went, except in the general direction of the enemy, but our shooting on the whole must have been good enough, for line after line of advancing Germans were stopped. The boys began digging in and I with my section moved off in the hope of finding our own battalion, my right shoulder aching like hell from the unaccustomed recoil of my rifle butt.'

For the next four months, as the Germans kept up their last desperate attempt to turn the tide of war, Chaney's division was moved up and down the fluctuating front, doing stop-gap jobs where the need seemed greatest. Casualties were heavy on both sides. Twice Chaney narrowly escaped death. His section of twenty men were mostly young, untried replacements sent straight from England. Looking back at that confused period he particularly remembers his first encounters with Australian and American troops.

During one chaotic retreat, on a road along which heavy siege guns were trundling behind their teams of sweating horses, whipped and cursed at by their drivers for not moving fast enough, he suddenly saw two horses come trotting smartly into view in the shafts of a swanky private carriage.

'Two Australians were sitting side by side on the driving seat, one wearing a black silk topper and flourishing a long whip, while the other held aloft an open umbrella. They stopped long enough to tell us that they had no intention of letting this smart equipage fall into German hands, saying "It's too good for the bleeding Hun". Then off they went, the driver raising his hat in salute, oblivious to all the shells that were falling around, some very close indeed. The man holding the umbrella shouted to us above the din that he was fortunate to have found it, and had opened it in the hope that it might keep off the rain —with a wink and nod indicating the shelling.

'Like most Aussies of that period they were quite mad, were the roughest of the rough, had no discipline at all, but were among the finest fighters in the world. At Villers Bretonneaux, where we had been rushed up to hold the line, they left the trenches altogether whenever Jerry opened up a heavy bombardment, while our orders were to stand and hold and put up with it. We did not think much of them at that time, even though they said they would be back later. The big blowers, we thought, all talk and no guts. But as soon as the shelling finished and it became dark, back they came. Leaving their rifles in the trenches they drew their bayonets from their scabbards and with a "How about it, digger?" and an answering "Righto, matey" they climbed over the top and disappeared into No Man's Land.

'It seemed hours later when they scrambled back into the trench, wiped their bayonets on the sandbags, grinned all over their faces and resumed trench duty as if nothing had happened. If we asked them what they had been up to, their answer was invariably "Just had ourselves a barney, matey". Of course there was one drawback to all this. Jerry would get mad at whatever they had been up to and slam us with everything, and once again there we crouched, taking it all, while the Aussies quietly flitted away with a casual "Be seeing you, digger".'

Chaney was less impressed with the Americans, who went into action for the first time in May 1918, and whose participation signalled the beginning of the end for Germany.

'The 33rd Chicago Regiment came under our special care, to be carefully initiated into the mysteries of war, but they had so much swank and bounce, they knew all there was to know, that I am afraid we did not take to them at all. Besides carrying rifles they also wore automatic pistols. They took one look at our revolvers and told us we looked like a bunch of cowboys with such out-of-date weapons, and we retorted by saying they had no idea how to carry a rifle properly. They were continually showing off their prowess by drawing their automatic pistols from the holsters as fast as possible and twirling them round and round on their trigger fingers. They were an uncouth, uninhibited, extrovert mob, never alluding to their regiment as the Thirty-third but always as "de Dirty Turd Chicago Boys".

'This was the only time I met up with the American Army and I think the experience tended to make my section and myself a little biassed. Possibly it was also because of the great contrast between us. They were all well built and well dressed, a fine upstanding lot of lads with plenty of bounce and an abundance of self-confidence, with good clean equipment, ready to take on anybody or anything. We veterans had become quiet and restrained, all the new lads coming to us from England were very young, almost untrained and on the whole of poor physique.'

But the occasion that most deeply affected Chaney came when his brigade had been pulled out of the line shortly after a gas attack by the Germans. 'We stayed for a day or two in a small village school, and my heart still aches when I remember parading for roll call, to get a check on how many of us were left. Just a handful of us faced the sergeant-major standing in front with sheets and sheets of paper, shouting out names one after the other. Any name not answered he called a second and third time, no answer and the name was crossed out. Occasionally there was a commotion in the ranks and a raising of an arm, causing someone to answer, "He's present sarn'-major, but he can't talk. It's the gas."'

Throughout the war Chaney never got used to death on the battlefield. 'It did not seem right, and sometimes I did not think it was possible to see a strong healthy fellow suddenly drop and become immediately useless. It was not fair to the same young men when they fell in grotesque and sometimes ugly attitudes, Scotsmen in their kilts being the most vulnerable in this respect. I remember thinking how disrespectful death

131

can be when I saw a Highlander hanging over the wire, his kilt thrown up over his back, exposing his bare buttocks to the sky. And there was disgust at the ugliness of death as the bodies swelled up like balloons, bulging out of their uniforms, sometimes smelling to high heaven.'

Such memories remained buried for many years after the war when Chaney, like so many others who had been promised a 'Land fit for Heroes', plunged into another kind of fight for survival. It was during the days of the Depression in 1928 that two particular memories began to haunt his dreams.

In one he saw again the face of the dead German with the spiked helmet, 'on his knees staring up at me as I had first seen him in May 1915, the man who, though dead, had made me feel fear for the first time'. In the second he went back to a forgotten occasion in November 1917 when he had been ordered by the adjutant to take a party of 'odd-bods' with rations, water and rum to troops holding out in Bourlon Wood on the Cambrai front.

'I took a compass bearing from our position and off we set— buglers, cooks, batmen—heads down, knees bent. It seemed ages, staggering along with our various loads, before we reached the advance posts and thankfully handed over our precious loads. The easiest way back was down a sunken road, but sunken roads are notoriously dangerous and we all knew it. When Jerry could not see what was going on down in a sunken road he had a habit of trying to blow it to pieces every few minutes. As we hurried down this road, strewn with equipment and dead bodies, we heard a voice calling for help.

'In the darkness we began searching around and eventually found, lying among a number of dead bodies in the ditch, a young soldier. I asked him what was wrong with him but all he could say was that he was unable to move. He did not know where he was wounded, all he knew was that he felt paralysed. Most of my party had hurried on. Even if we had been able to do anything for him, none of us wanted to stay in that road for a minute longer than necessary. By now the windiness of the others had got into me and it took me only a moment to leave him there. I would pass the word on to the nearest stretcher bearers, giving them his position. Making excuses for ourselves, we hurried on to the support troops, passed the information on and then, without giving it another thought, made a dash for our own headquarters.'

It all came back in Chaney's dream.

'I asked myself why. I had left many men, hundreds even, lying wounded and passed on—it was not possible to act as an ambulance man when one had another job to do. I had sent many men out on jobs from which they had never returned. But somehow this lad would repeatedly intrude into my subconscious. I began to worry about it, wondering had I been a coward and just left him there to die? Did I really tell the stretcher bearers exactly where he was lying? Had they found him and brought him in? Had he died up there? What must his feelings have been as we hurried down the road, leaving him lying there in pain, helpless?

'I made excuses for myself. My party had hurried on and I could not have moved him on my own. But it did not stop me from dreaming about him, week after week, month after month. Even today, although I do not know his name or regiment or even remember what he looked like, I still have a guilty feeling about him. My imagination sees him still lying there among the dead at the side of the sunken road.'

6   All for a Shilling a Day

'There is no finer fighter in the whole world than the British infantryman. I have seen them going past our guns on their way to a spell in the front line, possibly knowing that during that spell they would go over the top, to take prisoners perhaps, or to attempt to straighten out the line a little. What were their chances of survival? Not very high. But it didn't stop them singing or whistling as they went.

'I have seen this many times, and also the few only who passed us on their return. One day a fine man, the next a shattered body in No Man's Land. I really think that if the civilian people at home, in every country, could, even just once, have looked at shattered bodies lying on the muddy ground of No Man's Land, there would have been a stop to the war.'

William Pressey was a gunner in the Royal Artillery and most of his war was waged in gun emplacements some distance from No Man's Land. A gunner's life, as he describes it in his 48,000-word journal 'All for a Shilling a Day', was in many ways less harrowing than that of the infantryman he refers to with such admiration and pity. But death was often close. He was badly gassed during the battle for the Messines Ridge in 1917 and spent four months in Blighty. During the German offensive in 1918 his battery fought a hectic rearguard action for eight days as they retreated from St Quentin to Amiens, with no infantry between them and the pursuing Germans.

Pressey enlisted in January 1915 when he was 'eighteen and foolish and in a great hurry to get fighting'. He was a turner and fitter in the engineering trade but, on learning that his skills might be directed to a munitions factory, he gave his occupation as shop assistant. He regretted this when he realised that he could have been signed up in the Army Ordnance Corps, where he would have got a specialist's six shillings a day instead of the shilling he got as a mere gunner.

'All for a Shilling a Day' was written after his retirement as a millwright with the General Electric Company at Witton near Birmingham. 'I have many times been asked to shut up if ever I mentioned the War,' he writes. ' "We don't want to hear any of those stories," they said, so I did what I was told, all these years until now, and it has given me great pleasure to write this book for my daughter, who was one of the few who would listen to a war story.'

Pressey was early on singled out for his technical expertise. 'I knew and understood machinery and the other chaps didn't. They were like someone driving a car without understanding its working. But, after all, guns were just machines.' His story is centred on guns and the shells they fired, but he shows a constant awareness of what is going on just out of sight, men fighting men.

Trained on 18-pounders, he had graduated to 4.5 howitzers by the time he took part in his first major action, the Somme offensive in 1916. In the early hours of 1 July, his battery added its cacophony to the greatest bombardment yet launched.

'We were told that more shells were fired in that bombardment than in the whole war up till then and that every square yard of ground for about six miles would be hit by a shell. We expected our infantry would have only a little clearing up to do. But no. The Germans knew what was coming and withdrew their army right back, leaving pockets of machine gunners to kill as many of our lads as they could until they themselves were blotted out.

'Right from the start streams of ambulances, wagons and even farm carts with straw on the floor, trundled past our guns while we were firing away like mad, to fetch our wounded out. Now and then a few German wounded would pass us, being led by one of our lads, some smiling and giving the "thumbs up" sign, for they knew that for them the war was over. There were two of our boys leading one of their mates between them. He was a big, fine chap. He was trembling violently, could only stumble along, and was crying like a child. His nerves had gone.'

The casualness of death on the Western Front came home to Pressey some days later when his gun team lost their brightest spark, a tall Cockney of 20 named Symons. 'He was the comedian of our team, invaluable to our morale, and would crack a joke on the most miserable of occasions. His face would sort of wrinkle up when he laughed, and one was practically forced to laugh with him.'

The battery had moved forward to keep within range of the enemy and slit trenches had been dug near the guns in which to take shelter when retaliatory fire became heavy. Symons' job at the time was to lay the gun on target through the dial sight, a delicately made instrument so precious that it was also the layer's responsibility to lift it from its socket and dive with it to safety when the order to take cover was given.

' "Everyone under cover" came the cry and our team of four leapt from the gun into the trench like pennies into a kiddies' money box. As we did so Symons shouted, "Oh! The dial sight!" Before anyone could stop him he leapt out of the trench, took two strides and leaned forward with both hands to lift off the dial sight. As he did so another shell crashed. Symons turned and with a leap crashed on top of us, still clutching the dial sight. Our arms caught him as he landed, and we lowered him into the bottom of the trench. He had been hit in the back, and in seconds his face turned black and he was dead. No one spoke. We turned from each other to hide the tears, and they fall now as I write. He was a grand lad and a good soldier and the shock of losing him lasted a long time. No more would we laugh at his jokes. Losing him seemed like losing a brother. No other casualties ever affected us in the same way. And it was all for the safety of a damned dial sight.'

Like most front-line soldiers, Pressey looked at the war from the constricted circle of his own unit. Authority is portrayed by him as arbitrary, even inhuman. An abiding grievance was the fact that gunners had to walk behind their limbers.

'Although from the beginning of 1916 we were never in one place for very long and travelled many hundreds of miles altogether, we were never allowed to ride on the gun limbers and ammunition wagons, which had seats enough for a full gun team. Instead we had to fold our blankets and fasten them to the seats and, with overcoats, bandoliers and haversacks, march behind. Why? There were wire cages under limbers and wagons that could have held the blankets. It couldn't have been to save the horses—gun and limber could be moved by eight men fairly easily and there were six horses to do this. Was it to look smart? But often we were dragging our feet after a few miles and holding on to straps. Sometimes we would use the two metal seats on the gun itself—taking it in turns to dart forward on to the seats while the others kept watch. Usually we arrived dead tired at a new position, only to have to use pick and shovel throughout the night to get the guns into the gun pits and covered up before daylight.'

He has few kind words to say about the officers he served under. His bitterest memory is of a replacement major, 'with a very sour nature', under whose command he saw an offender undergo No. 1 Field Punishment.

'If a man was sentenced by court martial to this punishment he was tied or strapped to a gun wheel or wagon wheel. Legs spread out and ankles fastened to spokes of the wheel, and the same with wrists, like a crucifixion. Not to be able to move an inch became torture.

'I had to help to strap this man on. It was a freezing cold winter's day and we let him have overcoat, balaclava helmet and woollen gloves. But half an hour later this major strolled round, bellowed like a bull and ordered the overcoat, helmet and gloves removed. The man was there for an hour and a half and no one was allowed to speak to him or go near him. I took two chaps to fetch him in. He was almost frozen and we practically carried him back. He couldn't move arms or legs as the straps had been tightened by the major's orders—we had left them slack. As no officers were around we carried him to the cook-house. Plenty of pain, for as we loosened him and rubbed him, tears flowed from his eyes. And unprintable words from his mouth.'

For the private soldier at the front there were persistent hardships that had nothing to do with discipline, nor even with the enemy. Pressey elaborates on three that remain most vividly in his mind: hunger, vermin, exposure.

'My whole four years as a gunner I was hungry all the time. It must have taught me a lesson, for never through the remainder of my life have I ever grumbled at a poor meal. Behind the lines you could buy, if you had the money, bread, eggs, sweets, and sometimes have a meal in the back room of a shop. Our actual rations were only about half what they should have been. I believe that enough food to satisfy every soldier left the base. But the nearer it got to the battle area the less it got, being sold or stolen.

'If anyone had questioned the authorities they would have been told that every soldier got half a loaf of bread a day. We never got this once. Many, many times we had one slice only for breakfast and for tea hard biscuits. These were so hard that you had to put them on a firm surface and smash them with a stone or something. I've held one in my hand and hit the sharp corner of a brick wall and only hurt my hand. Iron rations all right. Sometimes we soaked the smashed fragments in water for several days. Then we would heat and drain, pour condensed milk over a dish-full of the stuff and get it down. It felt like a half-brick, but at least your stomach was full.'

Lice (or chats) were a constant preoccupation.

'At night you would strip off and kill them, counting as you did so. When you had killed a hundred exactly—even though you might have three or four hundred left—you ran a candle flame along all the seams of shirts and pants where they were white with lice eggs. They crackled slightly as the flame went along. Many shirts and pants have just fallen apart after some of this treatment. I had thin shirts and underwear sent out from home, easy to wash and dry. But after putting on a clean set, the next night one could start chatting. They were in your blankets, everywhere.

'In the depths of winter with frost and ice about we took it in turns to hang blankets and shirts outside. Two nights and days would kill the chats. Whoever's blanket was out would share someone else's bed and then change round. But we couldn't often hang anything out—even a handkerchief might be spotted by the Germans. It was a losing battle.'

Keeping from freezing in winter was another problem.

'Fellows would sleep two in a bed for warmth. I soon learned that to eat something—if there was something to eat—put more warmth in the body than sitting near a poor bit of fire. If you were not on some active work like filling sandbags you had to exercise in some way. Stamping the feet, deep breathing, moving the muscles. Or you could go so stiff with cold that you could hardly move when it was time to do so.

'You did all sorts of things to combat cold. Sandbags were tied round the legs, and old pieces of blanket. Then your over-coat, and over that the waterproof sheet you usually lay on. We blessed the old ladies at home who knitted woollen balaclava helmets to send us.'

It was on 7 June 1917, during the battle for the Messines Ridge, that Pressey was gassed.

'We had been shooting most of the night and the Germans had been hitting back with shrapnel, high explosive and gas shells. With the terrific noise and blinding flashes of gunfire, if a lull occurred for only a few minutes and you were leaning against something, you had just to close your eyes and you were asleep. Nearing daylight we were told to rest. We dived into the dugout, I pulled off my tunic and boots and was asleep in no time at all.

'I was awakened by a terrific crash. The roof came down on my chest and legs and I couldn't move anything but my head. I thought "So this is it, then". I found I could hardly breathe. Then I heard voices. Other fellows with gas helmets on, looking very frightening in the half light, were lifting timber off me and one was forcing a gas helmet on me. Even when you were all right, to wear a gas helmet was uncomfortable, your nose pinched, sucking air through a canister of chemicals. As I was already choking I remember fighting against having this helmet on.

'The next thing I knew was being carried on a stretcher past our officers and some distance from the guns. I heard someone ask "Who's that?" "Bombardier Pressey, sir." "Bloody hell." I was put into an ambulance and taken to the base, where we were placed on the stretchers side by side on the floor of a marquee, with about twelve inches in between. I suppose I resembled a kind of fish with my mouth open gasping for air. It seemed as if my lungs were gradually shutting up and my heart pounded away in my ears like the beat of a drum. On looking at the chap next to me I felt sick, for green stuff was oozing from the side of his mouth.

'To get air into my lungs was real agony and the less I got the less the pain. I dozed off for short periods but seemed to wake in a sort of panic. To ease the pain in my chest I may subconsciously have stopped breathing, until the pounding of my heart woke me up. I was always surprised when I found myself awake, for I felt sure that I would die in my sleep. So little was known about treatment for various gases, that I never had treatment for phosgene, the type I was supposed to have had. And I'm sure that the gas some of the other poor fellows had swallowed was worse than phosgene. Now and then orderlies would carry out a stretcher.'

Next day Pressey arrived at Portsmouth in a hospital ship, twenty-six months after he had last been in England.

'I suppose the newspapers had told of the Messines battle for there were lots of people at the docks to see the first casualties. With an arm round the shoulders of two orderlies, I stumbled slowly through the crowd. I heard one young girl say, "Oh dear, Mother, look at that poor boy." I was the only one near, so it was me she meant and well she may. I hadn't noticed that the trousers they had given me were at least six inches too short and the sleeves of the jacket the same. This, and the fact that I could only go slowly, gasping for breath, I suppose I really did look a poor boy.'

After three months of tender care in hospital, where he was visited by his fiancée, Pressey was sent to Ripon in Yorkshire.

'Here they sorted out those who could be made fit enough for soldiering again. It was an awful place—like being taken from heaven and plunged into hell. Drilling and exercising were controlled by physical training instructors who had practically no medical or surgical knowledge at all. To kill or cure seemed to be their aim.

'Every morning we were out in the fields, tunics off, braces off shoulders and shirts open to the waist. Someone would shout "Bad chests over here", "Bad arms over here", "Bad legs over here", until each instructor had a party of about forty strong. In my crowd—gas cases like myself, some with bronchitis or asthma, some who had been shot through the chest—we would start at walking pace, then the command "Trot" and we would do our best to run.

'The first time I thought I was passing out, with the pain in my chest I had almost forgotten. I stopped still and the other chaps ran past me until they were halted. The instructor ran over with a shout of "Hey you, what the bloody hell do you think you're playing at?" I was doubled up gasping for

141

breath. He went to catch hold of me but I pushed him away. The sergeant instructor ran over. "What's up?" he enquired. "He dropped out, sergeant" was the reply. "What's the matter with you?" he asked. "Gassed," I said, "and I may tell you that I won't have this running." "Oh you won't eh? Very well. Fall out and come with me to the MO and we'll bloody well see about that."

The doctor was sympathetic enough to have him put under another instructor, who allowed his group to walk until recovered if they were breathless after trotting. He was shocked by what he saw going on around him—'Fellows trying to run and practically dragging one leg along, an instructor shouting "Now come on, get those arms higher, higher I said", even pushing a chap's arm up until he nearly fainted'—and was thankful when he was passed out after six weeks. 'The MO explained to me that I was far from fit, but he was sure that if I went into civilian life now, and worked and slept in buildings I wouldn't last long. If I stayed in the Forces, where I'd be in the open air most of the time, I could get completely well again.'

Six months later at 2 am on 21 March 1918, Pressey was with one of two gun teams of his battery in an advanced position some ten miles in front of Amiens and within shooting range of St Quentin when the German offensive was heralded by a massive bombardment. A heavy shelling with gas was expected and his crew wore their gas helmets as they fired through the night on selected targets.

'At about 7 am the awful rain of shells eased off and we were able to take off our gas helmets, to our great relief. But soon after a shell dropped near and down went the sergeant, hit in a leg. The noise of machine guns nearly drowned his scream for help. We put him on a section of duckboard, blood running from a trouser leg, and carried him to the dressing station. Bob was a heavy chap and we were resting for a few minutes when an infantry colonel appeared. He glared at us. "Who the hell are you, and what are you doing here?" I explained that we had just brought in our wounded sergeant. "Get back to your guns or I'll put a bullet in the lot of you," he screamed. One look at his eyes, and I knew he would, too. "Come on, chaps," I said.

'As we crossed the road, or what was left of it, before reaching the guns, two infantry chaps hurried towards us, one supporting the other who had one arm just hanging on by a muscle. We guided them to the dressing station and reached the guns. No guns were firing from our side. Up the road hurried about a dozen infantry boys. "Come on, come on," they shouted. "Nothing can stop the bastards." They looked wild as they passed.

'As far as we could find out, all lines to our battery had been cut. The last order we had received, from our officer in his dugout, was to continue firing. We fired a round or two. The cook managed to make some tea which we had with bread and bully beef. More infantry boys passed. They said they had fired until the machine guns were red hot. They had slaughtered wave after wave of the Germans, but still they came on. When they left us it went very quiet, except for an occasional shell from the enemy.

'In the afternoon a Jerry plane flew over us a couple of times. We kept quiet and lay still beside the guns. On his next visit he sprayed around us with his machine guns, the bullets cutting the ground and pranging off the steel gun shield. We had stopped shooting for it would have pointed out where we were. An hour went by. Then "Here he comes" shouted the cook. And just like cowboys shooting at Indians through the wagon wheels we waited for him to dive. It was a novelty for our boys to use rifles—some had never used one before. He dived and rifle bolts being slid back and forth, shots of ours and his and the noise of his engines made a terrifying couple of minutes. But none of us was hit. Whether we hit him we never knew, but he didn't come back.

'There had been no shells fired from our side for a long time and we were aware that everybody had left us. There were eight of us counting the cook and batman. The only hope at the back of our minds was that the major would send up a couple of gun teams to try to get us out. All around us, as the day wore on, was deadly quiet. The rise of the land to about 300 yards in front of us prevented us from seeing the enemy and, thank goodness, him from seeing us. There were only ourselves between him and our batteries, wherever they now were.

'Our eyes rarely left the top of the ridge. We expected at any moment the ground to turn grey with thousands of their uniforms. Now we just talked of getting one or two of the bastards before they got us. We never thought or spoke of standing clear of the guns with our hands up. Funny now, when I think of it. They must have been stunned at the slaughter and so tired that they stopped just over the hill in front of us. After all their casualties that day, if they had seen us, even with our hands up, some trigger-happy guy would almost certainly have wiped us out.

'It was getting dusk when someone suddenly said "What's that over there?" About a mile behind us and to our left, in the fading light, it looked like movement of some kind. We watched and waited, our hearts fluttering. Then I could see it was a couple of gun teams and limbers. I got on a high spot and waved my arms like a windmill. They stopped near some trees. Then the NCO in charge galloped towards us. I recognised him as he got nearer and ran to meet him. It was Bombardier Cross from our battery, a friend of mine. He leapt from his horse and we held each other for a moment without a word. Then I said, "Get them up as quickly and quietly as you can."

'The two gun teams started towards him before he reached them. They chose all the soft ground so as not to make any noise. There were six drivers and all were understandably jittery. Apparently the major had given us and the two guns up as lost in the afternoon but Bombardier Cross had asked if he could take a couple of gun teams to see if there was any sign of life. As they had passed no troops or guns on their two-mile journey up to us, it seemed to them that they were just driving on to meet the Germans.

'We had just enough chaps to get the two guns out of their pits. Then, as soon as the second gun was out on the road and hitched up, someone's control broke down. Before one of our boys could climb on to a wagon seat—and there were seats for us all—away they went down the road, bumping and clattering over pieces of timber and all sorts of rubbish. We shouted and screamed, but no good. They soon disappeared from sight.

'Terrible words were invented in the next few minutes. We were also afraid that the clatter they made had drawn attention to us, and that soon the Jerries would come over the hill to investigate. We got our overcoats on, put our personal things in our haversacks and slung them on, together with water bottle, bandolier and gas helmet. Each man carried a rifle. "Ready, boys?" I asked. "Yes, Bill," they answered. "Come on, then, let's get home." And away we started on that perishing two mile walk.

'It was getting dark and foggy and we had gone perhaps a mile when a voice shouted "Halt". An infantry sergeant with a man either side of him came up to me. "You in charge of this lot?" he asked. "I am." "Who are you, what are you and where d'you think you're going?" he asked. I told him what had happened. All the time the rifles of the two men were pointing at us. He said, "That's all right, mate, your two guns went past here about half an hour ago." "What's your job here then?" I asked. Any stray men, from whatever infantry unit, he said, were to be collected, put in the trench behind him, and, with rifles and machine guns, wait for Jerry to advance and then blast him.

'I could see the newly dug trench and some of the fellows in it. I said "Cheerio, and all the best" to them, and we started off again. Where to? For all we knew the battery may have drawn further back. At least we were going in the right direction for the time being, but we were all very tired, mentally and physically, and our walk was not very steady. We walked on and on, now and again calling those drivers all the foul names we could think of. To think we could have ridden quietly back and here we were, slogging it out, and nearly put in that trench behind a machine gun. We never forgot what they did, and I believe they didn't either.

'At long last we could see the flashing of torches. Someone shouted "They're here, sir!" Soon our arms were going up and down like pump handles, with smacks on the back, too. We didn't know we had so many friends. The officers were there, too, and, blow me down, the major slapped me on the back, and led me away to tell him and the other officers all that had happened. We were all given food by the cook, followed by a stiff tot of rum.

'What Bombardier Cross had said to the major, or the major to him, when he got back with the guns but us left behind, I don't know. Cross got a Military Medal for volunteering to look for us. He felt badly about leaving us behind, and that medal seemed to come between us, for we were never close friends any more.'

For the next eight days there was no one between Pressey's battery and the Germans as they fell back on Amiens, firing as they went, themselves under shellfire. It was a chaotic time.

'A rider would gallop up with information as to where the enemy were. More map reading, and we start shooting. Same thing as before—shells dropping near us, limber up, then all of us hanging on like glue on gun limbers or wagons, for with drivers whipping their horses and wheels bumping over branches and shell holes you had to hang on or be tossed off. We would gallop for about a mile and then the officers in front would find a spot to put the guns, behind a hedge or in a sunken road or depression. We line up the guns ready to shoot again, while the cook tries to make tea without showing smoke, and we have something to eat. We slept under guns and wagons, with scouts out watching and listening for the Bosch sneaking up on us in the dark.

'One morning a scout galloped up saying there were Uhlans, German cavalry, on our left and right trying to get round the back of us. Limber up and away. But this time there were not only shells bursting but for the first time machine gun bullets. Some pranged off the wagons, but only one man had a bullet in his leg. Mystery—where did they come from? Little did we know that the Uhlans were now armed with mounted machine guns, not relying on their lances any more.

'There was no sign of life in farms and houses. Everyone must have fled before we got there. When we were not expecting to shoot we would go in search of food. In some places there was food half-eaten on the table, clothes piled up and finally not taken. In one small town where we had stayed a couple of months before there was an estaminet where we had been charged outrageous prices, possibly because the Americans and Canadians had been there. It was empty, like the rest of the town, and we ran down into the cellar and came out with our arms full of bottles of every description, including champagne. Wherever a shell had been taken out of an ammunition wagon, a bottle was now put in its place. By the time we moved off my gun team had around thirty bottles with us.

'It seemed that our officers either didn't know what was going on, or didn't care. At our next stop, after getting our guns ready to shoot, there was quite a bit of drinking and singing going on. My section officer walked over. "What the hell is going on, Pressey? It looks to me as if they're nearly all drunk." "They are, sir," I replied. "Wherever did they get it?" he asked. I told him, but not how many bottles we had. I said "Would you care for a drop, sir?" "Only if you can spare it," he said. "If you wait here, sir, I'll see what I can do." I didn't want him to see where we had it hidden. I walked over to my boys and said, "All right if I give Mayne a bottle?" "Just as you

147

like, Bom," they said. I went round the gun and got out two bottles without him seeing me. When I gave him two whole bottles he was off to share them as pleased as a schoolboy. That day I should say there were only about six of us capable of shooting until the boys had slept it off. Fortunately we didn't need to until next morning, when we let Jerry have two hundred shells or more before we pulled out again.

'All the time the thought at the back of our minds was where we were heading for. We knew we were being driven towards the coast. If we got there would ships be waiting for us and, if so, could we get away before his guns blew us out of the water? Where on earth were all our infantry and artillery?

'Nearing Amiens we passed farms with people standing outside the gates, hanging on to their homes until it seemed hopeless. Some had carts, others great bundles on their backs. I saw an old man pushing a very large and very old barrow, his aged wife sitting in it with a great pile of household things heaped round her so that you did not see her at first. The major stopped us, said something to these people, then called to us to get them on if we could. As the general service wagons were with us, we were able to pile on all who wished to ride with us. The old couple were lifted on, barrow and all. We didn't look like the battery that had been shooting that morning.

'Soon we could see the tall buildings of Amiens in front of us. Suddenly someone shouted, "Look over there—and over there ..." On both sides of the road and stretching as far as you could see, were guns, guns and still more guns. Guns of all sizes. Oh, how our hearts leapt at the sight. Then from all sides ran soldiers, mostly artillery. They took off their hats, waving and cheering as we passed. Oh, it was just grand. "Go and rest boys," they shouted, "and leave him to us." Some of our boys shed tears at this. I don't think anyone noticed mine.

'We dropped the French people off at a large building—there seemed to be some French officials there to look after them. And on we travelled, now looking more like a battery, to a place outside the town. We had lost nearly half our men. But, with all our six guns intact, we reckoned we had come out of the retreat from St Quentin rather well.'

Battered by the massed artillery, already decimated and exhausted by their advance, the Germans did not take Amiens. Though breakthrough attempts were made on other parts of the front and, at one stage, they were able to shell Paris less than seventy miles away, it was the turn of the tide. But bitter fighting continued through the next months as they were slowly rolled back, and Pressey's battery, brought up to strength again, was often in the thick of it.

On leave in October, he got married at Birmingham Register Office, honeymooning at Matlock. 'Although I had been engaged for a long time, I wouldn't marry until I saw the end of the war in sight. As this was the position now we did not wait any longer—especially as married couples received twelve shillings a week . . .'

On the morning of 11 November, Pressey was in a field repairing two guns.

'We had parts of the guns laid out on sacks. The fighting was still going on, but had left us behind. Then our section officer called for me. "Take it easy, Pressey," he said, "we'll not shoot again. An Armistice was signed at 11 o'clock." "Thank you, sir," I said. And I walked slowly back to my chaps. "What's up?" they asked. "It's all over," I replied. Then, instead of rejoicing, there was a flow of language. Why the bloody hell couldn't we have chased him right through Berlin while we had the chance . . .?

'Afterwards we heard of the tremendous rejoicing of the people at home—workers walking out of factories, parties, bonfires in the streets. Far, far different from our own reaction. It was very odd when I think about it that no one seemed over-joyed that the War was over.'

Pressey has written a 13,000-word sequel to his war journal, 'The Land Fit for Heroes—some memories of one man's struggle for survival after the fighting was over'. It is an often bitter account of the search for jobs—'Often I was as hungry as I was during the war years'—and the dulling preoccupation with advancement and making ends meet. Pressey must typify many less articulate veterans of the Great War now in retirement, looking back on those fighting days and finding them, for all the horrors and hardships, more meaningful, more alive, than any that have intervened.

One vividly remembered episode in the journal seems to sum up the conflicting aspects of the war—the excitement as well as the danger, the courage and sacrifice, above all the camaraderie and *esprit de corps* that kept men going even in the jaws of death. 'Theirs not to reason why, Theirs but to do and die . . .'

It happened during the retreat from St Quentin, at which time Pressey's division was operating on the extreme right of the British line where it linked up with the French.

'On the morning of the fifth day we had seen Uhlans on either side of us and had got out in a flaming hurry. Shells followed us as we had a hectic gallop through a village and dropped to a walk on going over a hill. Out of sight of the Germans over this hill we were walking along when we saw an unforgettable sight.

'Coming towards us were a troop of French cavalry. I should say a hundred and fifty or two hundred strong. Gosh, but they looked splendid. I think word must have got to them about the German cavalry harassing us and they had come to put a stop to that. They could never have been told about the machine guns. They laughed and waved their lances at us, shouting "Le Bosch fini". What a picture they made with sunlight gleaming on their lances. We slowed down as they trotted briskly past, and everyone was looking back at them.

'Before reaching the top of the hill they opened out to about six feet between each horse and in a straight line. We hardly breathed. Over the top of the hill they charged, lances at the ready.

'There was not a sound from us. Then, only a few seconds after they disappeared, the hellish noise of machine guns broke out. We just looked at each other. The only words I heard spoken were "Bloody hell . . ." That's what it must have been over that hill, for not one man came back. Several of their horses did, and trotted beside us, and were collected at our next stopping place.

'If only the cavalry officer had stopped for one minute and talked to our officers they would have told them of the mounted machine guns, and that it was certain death over the hill from where we had come. Who had sent that splendid troop to certain death? Surely all the conditions should have been known before sending lances against machine guns. If they were known, did anyone think the Germans would leave their machine guns and fight evenly, lance to lance? What an awful waste of husbands, brothers, sons. Many commanders of the War must have a lot on their minds.'

7 Gallipoli - the Great Beyond

There was an almost festive air aboard the 7,000-ton hospital ship *Delta*, gleaming white with large red crosses painted either side, as she sailed the blue waters of the Mediterranean in the late summer of 1915, eastward bound for a destination still only guessed at by the 600 passengers. They comprised three field ambulance brigades, and among the doctors, most of them new to khaki, was a young Canadian, Norman King-Wilson, a ship's surgeon before the war, now beginning a diary of what he excitedly foresaw as 'a great adventure'.

'There were British, Canadians, South Africans, and New Zealanders aboard—men from every corner of the Empire', he recalls in the 35,000-word journal he later wrote up from those diary jottings. 'We had for fellow passengers a score of Red Cross sisters, with whom the more susceptible of our number never tired of flirting. In the evenings we gambled and sang boisterous songs to the alleged melody given forth by an unfortunate piano—unfortunate because it was thumped so hard and also because its top was the favourite seat of big Ross, the Scottish footer international. The songs we sang were mostly NOT of Arcady, but we were young men, going out to the great beyond, to we knew not what, so we did "eat, drink and be merry" to the consternation of a few elderly and dignified gentlemen, who did not yet comprehend that we were going to see strange lands and sights.'

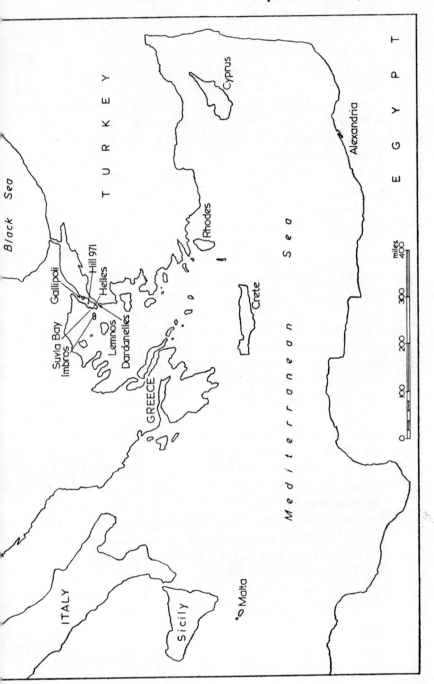

What King-Wilson was to see was the final phase of the eight-and-a-half months' campaign in Gallipoli, as harrowing in its way as anything experienced on the Western Front. As a doctor he was more concerned with the ravages caused by suffocating heat and plagues of flies, by violent storms and freezing cold, than by Turkish shells and bullets. 'The entire army is feeling and looking ill'', he wrote towards the end.

The Gallipoli campaign, basically aimed at forcing the Dardanelles, capturing Constantinople and opening a back door into Germany, was—and still is—the most controversial campaign of the war. It has variously been described as an unmitigated disaster, badly planned and ineptly executed, and an inspired enterprise that came near to hastening victory. King-Wilson rarely alludes to the handling of the campaign, not even to the lamentable inadequacies of the medical services. Himself a sick man when he was among the last to creep through the darkness for the final stealthy evacuation from Suvla Bay, his abiding memories are of the men who endured the nightmare—'exhausted, disease-smitten wrecks whom people at home call vaguely "heroes" '—and of the epic grandeur of the setting in which they fought, ancient as Troy. For all the hardships and horrors, the excitement with which he embarked on his 'great adventure' never quite leaves him.

It was on 7 August that the *Delta* anchored off the island of Imbros, ten miles from the Gallipoli peninsula, the day after a big new attack had been launched, involving the landing of 20,000 fresh troops at Suvla Bay. The attack, in which a total of some 50,000 Allied troops were engaged, was designed to end the stalemate that had existed since shortly after the initial landings on 25 April. That it failed was again due to bungling leadership rather than to the courage and tenacity of the fighting men. Within three days the stalemate had resumed, at a cost of over 18,000 Allied casualties.

From Imbros King-Wilson could hear the distant boom of the guns, but it was to be some weeks yet before he set foot on that blood-soaked shore. The urgent problem now was the care of the wounded flooding back from that unseen battleground in much greater numbers than had evidently been envisaged. King-Wilson's account of the nightmare voyage of a hospital transport to Alexandria is indicative of the lack of adequate foresight and preparation that marked so much of the campaign. The evacuation of the wounded and sick—a total of nearly 22,000—continued until 13 August by which time all available hospitals in Egypt and Malta were full up and the surplus had to be shipped back to England in any transports available.

King-Wilson found himself aboard the *Caledonia*, a liner without Red Cross protection, together with five of his fellow-medicos, a matron and six sisters. By now they were aware of what was going on and were expecting heavy casualties, but for King-Wilson, particularly after the carefree jollifications of the past weeks, his first contact with the realities of war had a stunning effect.

'It was a shock to me when four lighters pulled up alongside and we saw the poor shattered figures, with bloody bandages, grimy faces and dirty clothes, who were crowded together below us. Each lighter had a MO in charge doing his best but men were dying every minute. Now we started to bring them aboard, some walking, some on stretchers, some on a comrade's back, others lifted up by the ship's crane and deposited with great care on deck or down one of the hatches into a hold.

'We had arranged that all BAD cases go down to a certain hold, officers to 1st class cabins and music room, and that every man be ticketed and numbered as he came on, and so amid a babel we got the poor chaps aboard—British, Australian, Sikhs and Gurkhas, laying them on pallisades, where most fell asleep at once, the dead all being placed together in the ship's hospital, under lock and key—the final sleep of all.'

By the time the *Caledonia* weighed anchor, there were 1,350 wounded of all ranks aboard. King-Wilson had been appointed ship's adjutant and was responsible for some 200 wounded in the officers' wards and upper deck, with one sister to assist him.

'We worked until we could no longer tell what we were seeing or doing, dressing, dressing, dressing, hour and hour on end, all day and night, picking out the cases where the dreaded "gas gangrene" had set in, and where immediate and high amputation was the only hope of saving life. Even the clean open decks stank of the horrid smell of gangrenous flesh and the holds, dark, hot and ill-ventilated, were just like the cockpits of the fleet in the days of Nelson.

'The operating theatre in the 2nd class smoke room, despite the valiant efforts of McCasey and the theatre sister, was a stinking, bloody shambles, where patients were brought up on a stretcher and left waiting for their predecessor to be taken down, then rapidly chloroformed (no ether whatever), placed on the table and leg or arm whipped off in a couple of minutes by a circular incision, one sweep of the knife and the bone sawed through, the limb thrown into a basket with many others, awaiting incineration. No sutures were used, just a huge moist dressing applied to the stump, then, his work completed, McCasey, bloody and perspiring in the muggy tropical night, would await the next poor victim of German ambition.

'We did not realise when the ship raised anchor or where she went, the whole voyage was a nightmare. Even the Parson was busy, for every night, at midnight exactly, he would appear in surplice and cassock on the main deck aft and there, by the flickering light of a solitary candle lantern, would read aloud the burial service. It was the most weird ceremony one could possibly imagine—lying on the deck, bound tightly up in sailcloth, with a weight at the feet, anything from three to near a score of silent motionless figures, three placed at a time on the gangway board from the ship's bulwark, lying feet pointing seaward, the Union Jack spread over all three, the hundreds of dark figures watching from the ship's decks, sailors and soldiers, silent and awed for once at the sight of the last rites of those chaps who so lately had been cheery lusty comrades.

'The few words of the chaplain soon over, the Jack is whipped off the bodies by a sailor and three bells are heard in the engine room, the great engines stop their roar and the ship glides on in silent darkness, the board is elevated and, with a swish, followed by a dull splash, THOSE three join Britain's countless dead deep down in the Aegean Sea.

'Not being a registered hospital ship, we travelled of course in darkness by night and in constant dread of submarines by day, but as we had a speed of seventeen knots we were able to outstrip any had we sighted them. The sisters used to look very quaint and old-fashioned going about at night with candle lanterns through the long dark corridors. The wounded officers and men were mostly cheery as could be and many a little tale came out, of the fight on the thrice won and finally lost crest of Hill 971, Sari Bair, which was supposedly the key of the peninsula. The grit and endurance of these men was remarkable and the more slightly injured helped to the best of their ability the helpless ones.

'At long last we reached Alexandria. We had only been about four full days en route but it seemed interminable. There were about forty deaths and sixty amputations and the entire staff was utterly exhausted. We docked immediately on arrival and a long line of ambulances awaited us on the great Pier to convoy direct to the splendid hospitals where every care would be given. I cannot leave this part of my tale without remarking on the scrupulous cleanliness of the Gurkhas we had aboard. They, poor chaps, were the only men who made any attempt at cleaning up, brushing their hats and cleaning their rifles and beloved *kukris*, those short, curved, broad-bladed knives with which these childlike black warriors dispatch their victims. The Sikhs on the other hand were not nearly as cheery as their compatriots and were miserable objects to behold. It was with thankful hearts that we saw the last of that cargo.'

After four days spent refitting and taking on fresh medical and surgical supplies, the *Caledonia* was loaded with 1,200 fresh troops, mostly Yeomanry who had been training in Egypt, and King-Wilson and his fellow-medicos was kept busy injecting them with anti-cholera serum as they sailed to Mudros, the great natural harbour on the island of Lemnos, which was headquarters of the General Staff.

'One could readily believe that half the shipping of the world was anchored at Mudros, of every size and shape, from the dapper little pinnaces of the Dreadnought to the gigantic *Mauretania*, waiting there—yes, waiting, at vast expense until their time should come to be loaded or unloaded with troops or beef or what not for the great "show", the "Gamble" at Gallipoli. The key to this puzzle (which caused Lord Kitchener to say "Mudros is a tragedy") was the RMSP *Aragon*, anchored there at a cost of £6,000 per month rental as a comfortable summer home for the General Staff who directed the Gamble. Why they were not housed ashore and the valuable transport released for more worthy service, God knows, but, while I do not usually grouse, the very name of the *Aragon* stank. Officers reporting for duty or orders to the *Aragon* were kept waiting hour after hour, and it was with difficulty that they could buy a meal. Why officers reporting should have to buy sustenance passes comprehension but this was the fact and just part and parcel of the treatment meted out to any poor mortal who had to report there.

'We were in Mudros for four days and my journey ashore to the medical stores for more supplies gave me the first insight into the awful conditions of active service in the east. Officers and men looked thin, white and listless, and carried fly whisks to rid themselves momentarily of that awful pest. A layer of sand and dust covered everything. White-faced officers sat in tents and groused, perspired and swore, and the men lived nearby in veritable dog kennels made of bits of boxes, tarpaulins, tin, etc.

Oh, Mudros was a ghastly, dysentery infested hole, the very worst place I have ever seen.'

Most of the 1,000 Gallipoli casualties with whom King-Wilson now sailed the 3,000 miles back to England were sick rather than wounded. He spent a short leave with his wife, 'wandering about the beautiful Chiltern hills, drinking into my soul the green peace of the English fields and hedges'. On 13 September he sailed from Plymouth, with 1,200 troops aboard, in the *Lake Manitoba*, the CPR liner on which he had made his first voyage as a ship's surgeon in 1910. Two weeks later he was back at Mudros, where orders awaited him to report immediately to the 88th Field Ambulance on Gallipoli. It was with an excitement the keener for having been so long delayed that the same night he approached the menacing bulk of Suvla Bay aboard a 'beetle', the armour-plated landing barge used to get troops and stores ashore.

'We drew silently in amongst the other shipping, under the shadow of those looming hills, from all parts of which showed points of light, some flickering signals, some quite still, some others just sudden white flashes, followed a minute later by a muffled report. We landed along slippery planks across rolling lighters until we reached a strip of sand in the glare of two acetylene lamps. A crackle of musketry was because news of our advance in France on 26 September had just reached the trenches and our men raised a cheer all along the line whereupon the Turks, fearing an attack, commenced a heavy fusillade.

'I spent the night in a stone quarry and awoke at 6 am. Everywhere about us in the already brilliant sunshine myriads of men and mules were toiling at landing and piling stores of all sorts, from guns to jam—an unforgettable scene of labour, the thin brown ragged khaki-clad men, and officers scarcely discernible from them, working like ants, and away in the distance, ending with the universal sand coloured landscape, yet more toilers. Not a tree to be seen on West Beach, barely a bit of scrub which we afterwards found covered most of the hillsides.'

To contact the 88th Field Ambulance Brigade, King-Wilson was directed to 'the topmost tent' on the crest above the bay. 'I was told not to expose myself too long on the crest but could not resist gazing from this eminence at the battlefield known as Suvla Bay. Spread out before me in a panorama was a great plain, bounded on the west by the sea. The southern limit was a vast mountain wall, ending abruptly at the sea and running far inland, the summit of which was known as Sari Bair, technically Hill 971. The plain had an area of roughly ten square miles and I gazed with wonder at that little patch of land which had already cost so many thousands of lives and on which I knew unseen armies lay entrenched.'

After going down into the plain to a forward station to report to his new CO, Lt-Colonel Gostling, 'a tall brown emaciated man in short sleeves constantly dusting himself with a fly whisk', he returned to the encampment on the crest to await his fellow-officers.

'With field glasses glued to my eyes I drank in every feature of the landscape. Bright shafts of light reflected from many places, these I found came from biscuit tins and on hill sides one could see lines of little burrows, housing an army. But there was extraordinarily little to be seen.

'When the others arrived I was struck with the worn-out look of the men, sallow and hollow-eyed, and they worked very slowly indeed. At 4 o'clock tea was announced in an operating tent where they had rigged up a table and some boxes and camp chairs and the four of us sat down to a very respectable tea of jam, bread and butter, tea, sugar and condensed milk. Just as tea started I heard a rapidly approaching noise, between a whistle and a roar, seemingly coming straight for our tent. I was pouring milk into my tea at the moment and glanced at the other faces about me, and, seeing merely a momentary attitude of strained listening, I decided that my cue was to watch them and keep quiet, but though I did not show it it was a strained moment for me. The thing passed overhead with a horrible scream and burst on impact on the hillside near Army HQ, 100 yards away. It was my first shell and never will I forget that weird experience. One feels like crawling into a worm hole for shelter and never coming out. The tent we sat in had many holes in it, produced chiefly by shrapnel.

'As dusk fell the crackle of musketry and machine guns grew into a considerable din, continuing with bursts of fire until dawn, and one watching from the hillside would see frequent flashes of Very white light from the direction of the trenches followed a few seconds later by a very sharp report—these were bombs. Next morning I was awakened by that loathsome pest the fly. Flies I could never get used to, crawling in one's food, swimming in one's soup. sticking in one's jam, it was horrible. If we were eating bread and jam it was a race to get it in one's mouth before the flies got entangled—to me the fly pest was the worst hardship of the campaign.'

That morning King-Wilson had his first close look at a dressing station down in the plain.

'It was in a "nullah", or dried up water course, 20 feet wide at the top and 8 feet deep. It looked and smelt what it was, a slimy sink, alive with flies, turtles and crawling things of all descriptions. A little marsh grass grew about and a few tiny pools of smelling water, alive with frogs and turtles, were to be seen at the bottom of the "nullah". In holes rudely cut into the eastern bank, in little dens built out of rotting sand bags, and in hollows where the damp showed through, were living an officer and thirty-five men. Thirty feet away a "stink" hole full of vermin feeding on the body of a dead mule, no shade from the pitiless sun, and flies, flies everywhere—such was the dressing station.

'Any poor unfortunate patients were laid in the bottom of the "nullah" where a few sand bags had been built up at either end, and which was ironically called "The Hospital". The man in charge was a Lt Andrews, a fairly plump and quite self-satisfied little man. He was lying on a stretcher propped up on two empty boxes, between two rows of sandbags with a fly net for a roof. He asked us in and hospitably offered tea. Here at last I was seeing what I had imagined active service to be. The tea was vile. We had for three of us two greasy tin cups and one greasy enamel bowl and apricot jam spread on "biscuits hard and dry" and flies boiled and raw.

'Later men began to troop into the dressing station, some with kits, mostly without, but all dirty, brown, listless, hollow-eyed and emaciated—these were the elimination of the MO's morning sick parades in the trenches—the men who were no longer able to "carry on," and they looked it as they lay there in any available spot of shade. They lay passive, sleeping or dozing, the flies settling in black patches on the dirty parts of their clothing, on their faces and hands, yet they did not even have energy to brush them away. They were poor, half-dead, semi-conscious wrecks of humanity who had until an hour back been on duty in the trenches. They were merely the WORST of the morning sick parade, perhaps twenty per regiment.

'Practically speaking my work consisted in eliminating the dysentric cases from those who had merely diarrhoea. The dysentery cases were ticketed and sent to the casualty clearing station 600 yards from the Turks, and all that lay between me and them was a few hundred men, exhausted, disease smitten wrecks whom people at home call vaguely "heroes" and whom we out there knew were Privates Smith, Brown and Atkins, blaspheming and "sticking it".'

When, on 2 November, King-Wilson was put in charge of the dressing station he did what he could to improve conditions, marking out places for a cook house and latrines and en-larging the "hospital" and men's dugouts. The proportion of sick to wounded was now eight to one, and it was fatiguing work, not helped by the fairly persistent whine with 'the occasional "smack" when a tree was hit or "phut" as they struck the earth.' A three-day spell of duty at a dressing station was regarded as sufficient and King-Wilson looked forward to the periods back at the base camp.

'It was always a source of delight to me to sit in the door of my tent and watch through my field glasses the happenings on the beaches, the goings and comings of ships far out to sea, and then to pick up details in the Turkish lines—Chocolate Hill, which I knew thronged with men, looked exactly like an ant hill magnified, the dugouts showing their openings towards the sea. The sunsets were gorgeous and the glassy sea with warships and transport and smaller vessels dotted about, some in the distance leaving long black streaks on the horizon, were objects of fascination. The banked up clouds reflected the most wonderful glories of colour from darkest purple to faintest pink, and often patches of wonderful crimson. The sun would sink behind Imbros whose beetling crags were sharply outlined against the splendour of the sky so that it seemed so near one could scarcely believe it was ten miles away.

'Sometimes in the evening several of us would climb to the top of Karakol Dagh and sit quietly drinking in every detail of the wonderful panorama spread before us, and, in the setting sun, we could see the faint outline of Mount Athos in Greece, ninety miles away. Then as dusk deepened the sound of myriads of creaking mule carts rose out of the plain, and the weird Oriental chants of the Sikh muleteers, singing the praises of some long departed heroes of the East. Then suddenly the crackle of musketry from the lines and the white flash of bombs with their sound coming up long after, out of the stillness, and we were reminded that night, and the horrors of war, were upon us.'

On 23 November Colonel Gostling was so ill with dysentery and jaundice that he could not carry on and asked King-Wilson to 'ticket' him and have him sent away. Wilson became temporary CO and immediately set about making improvements to the clearing station facilities, having particularly in mind the pending winter, about which dire rumours had been circulating among the troops. The weather broke on the evening of 26 November.

'The wind from the north-east had risen and every tent was straining on its guy ropes and men could be heard hammering pegs in all directions. A foreboding of evil seemed to come to all. For weeks we had heard of the dreadful winters on Gallipoli and anxiously watched the banked-up clouds and the ships tugging at their anchors in the Bay. By ten pm the wind was a positive gale. We all turned in early, making ourselves as snug as possible to keep out of the awful wind and cold and by midnight the rain came, not gently as from a soft grey English sky but in buckets, hurtled down from the massed black clouds and accompanied by thunder and lightning. Soon little trickles of water began to creep into the best-drained tents and the rain beat through the old sun-baked canvas in a driving mist, soaking everything.'

For the men in the trenches it was the start of a terrible ordeal.

'Trenches were six to eight feet deep in water and mud and men by the score were found drowned. But everywhere one was met not by grumbling or whines but by jests and good cheer as the poor half starved, half drowned men came down for their bit of refreshment. I saw seven Worcesters sitting on the parapet of a flooded trench singing "A life on the ocean wave", and everywhere heard jests, as "Now I s'pose we'll 'ave the blinkin' Nivy sailen up these 'ere canals, Bill", or " 'ope there ain't no submarines in these 'ere waters". Good old Worcesters, Essex and Hants, men of the Old Army, dirty scrubby cheery unpretentious dauntless heroes, every one. Sick at heart I turned to plough my way back to camp, feeling impotent. We could fight the Turk and his German masters but the first rainstorm of the winter had defeated us.

'By the night of the 27th the cold was bitter, the rain had ceased and the mud was rapidly freezing. We made a lean-to shelter on one side of the dry masonry compound Colonel Gostling had had built round his tent and placed our patients there where it was quite warm and dry. Dozens of old biscuit tins with holes knocked in them served as braziers in which we burned coke brought in sacks from the Beach. At the relief stations hundreds of men were having their feet, swollen to double their size, blue and stone cold, rubbed in oil. The pain must have been frightful but seldom did one hear a groan. The small aid posts in the trenches had some shocking cases brought in. Some frozen and unconscious, some quite drunk, for they had consumed large quantities of rum to keep warm. Some lying prone in the mud, dead. Oh God, it was pitiful.

'As the day wore on more and more men with frozen feet came hobbling down, some with rifles as crutches, some crawling, others being assisted by pals nearly as crippled as themselves. One officer was making his way slowly across the mud flat to our dressing station. He asked two others with him to go on and sat down in the mud. They went on, sending back bearers. When these reached him he was dead—of cold and exhaustion. I saw a corporal and two men of the 4th Worcesters come down from a redoubt called Dublin Castle three-quarters of a mile away through trenches filled with mud and ice carrying a machine gun, tripod and ammo belts. These they laid down on a tarpaulin they had brought, then had their boots and socks removed and feet rubbed, while they had hot soup, bully and biscuits. As all three had partially frozen feet and hands, I told them to go down to the dressing station but the corporal said "No, sir, we're going back to Dublin Castle, we left it all alone". So they picked up their gun and tripod and started back. How could I restrain them? They knew where their duty lay, they knew their own endurance and they went. Many men get VCs for acts done in the heat of action, but those men got nothing but the sense of duty done. Of such was the Old Army. Our total losses in three days were 600 drowned or died from exposure, and 6,000 casualties, mostly trench feet.'

On 10 December King-Wilson presented himself to the MO on a hospital ship in the bay. He had come for drugs to dull the acute pain he had been suffering from a rectal abscess forming. The pain continued, even when his mind was clouded with morphia, but now he had a challenging duty to occupy him. On 11 December he was told in secret that Gallipoli was to be evacuated. With the four officers and seventy-five NCOs and men of the 88th Field Ambulance Brigade under his command, he was to remain to the end.

The gradual withdrawal of 80,000 men from Suvla and Anzac, together with mules, vehicles, guns and stores, was the one major operation on Gallipoli that went without a hitch. Helped by a spell of settled weather, it was achieved by meticulous timing and elaborate subterfuges to deceive the Turks into thinking all was going on as usual.

'As the men withdrew, the old camps and roads were strangely silent and deserted, though at nights as usual long strings of GS carts creaked and groaned over the plain, star shells flared and musketry rattled, and we hoped and prayed that the Turks did not know that but a few hundred men lay between them and victory. We kept the lights lit in the deserted shelters on the hillside and I kept men moving up and down and round the camp all day long.'

By the night of 18 December, penultimate night of the evacuation, more than half the men had left.

'All the remainder of the 29th Division was now in the second line, the first line being held by merely 200 picked volunteers. They spent their time walking up and down the trenches, firing at birds to keep them from settling, sniping rapidly here and there, talking loudly at night, making smoke, sending up flares and even bombing and trying to represent an army. One officer, hearing a heated discussion on the far side of a traverse, went to investigate, thinking several of the men, forgetting the gravity of their position, had foregathered for a social hour. To his utter amazement on peeping around the edge of the traverse he found but one man, who was arguing and strafing, all to himself, in all the known dialects of the British Isles.

'On the morning of the 19th I got my final orders. By 8 pm only eleven men and myself of the FA remained. The men in the trenches spent the last day turning every dugout into a death trap and the most innocent looking things into infernal machines. Some dugouts would blow up when the doors were opened. A drafting table had several memorandum books lying on it each with electrical connections to an explosive charge sufficient to destroy a platoon. A gramophone, wound up and with record on, ready to be started, was left in one dug out so contrived that the end of the tune meant the death of the listeners. Piles of bully beef tins, turned into diabolical engines of destruction, lay scattered about. In front of the trenches lay miles of trip mines. Hundreds of rifles lay on the top of the parapet, with string tied to trigger, supporting a tin can, into which water from another tin dripped. Flares were arranged in the same way. Really I never thought the British Tommy possessed such diabolical ingenuity.

'That evening the 4th CCS officers and myself dined well on supplies left for us. We had a roaring fire in a big dugout, burning someone else's house. We laughed and yarned and jested, waiting, waiting for God knows what, but for something to break the silence that oppressed that vast empty graveyard, not only the graveyard of thousands of good men, but of England's hope in the Dardanelles. The hills seemed to tower in silent might in the pale, misty moonlight, and the few lights upon them flickered like the ghosts of the army that had gone. Up in the lines, from the "last Ditchers", rifles crackled and flares went up.

'Nine o'clock, and we knew the last men had left the trenches and were coming down. 9.30 and my eleven men and I, all our belongings on our backs, marched silently to the rendezvous at Y point. As I reported to the Staff Officer there, I could dimly see the head of a long column coming down Gibraltar Road in absolute silence, rags round their accoutrements, not a cigarette or pipe alight. Then commenced the waiting, at fever heat, while every man was accounted for. At eleven word came to move down to embark. Silently the hundreds rose, shouldered their kits and moved out. Down through piles of stores, jam, biscuits, bacon, black and saturated with petrol and paraffin ready for the torch. Down through the sunken road.

'Then the long minutes of suspense as we waited, huddled up, expecting at any moment a burst of fire. Out in the bay loomed the dim shapes of our guardian angels, four battleships. At last our time came and, at midnight exactly, we embarked on the packet *Red Breast*, on which were crowded nearly 2,000 men.

'She moved out immediately. Oh how strange to think it was all over. Suvla Bay was, for us, no more. Our little homes in the plains and in the hills were empty and silent. Yet the flares still flickered, the rifles popped. The saddest thought of all was of the lonely little cemeteries scattered in profusion all over the plain, last resting places of the men of the army who STILL held Suvla Bay.'

Total Allied casualties during the Gallipoli campaign have been estimated at 265,000, of whom some 46,000 were killed in action or died of wounds or sickness. King-Wilson was himself lucky to have survived. From Suvla Bay he was landed, with troops of the 29th Division, at Helles, the Allies' last foothold on the peninsula. The evacuation from here of the last 35,000 men was carried out in much the same way as that at Suvla and Anzac, and with equal success. But by now King-Wilson was too sick to be alert to it all. When he was taken aboard a transport bound for Alexandria on 9 January 1916, he was in the second week of typhoid fever, with a temperature of 102.

After three weeks in hospital in Alexandria, he returned to England in a hospital ship, this time as a patient. When, on 25 February, he was admitted to No 3 London General Hospital, mere thankfulness at being alive marked the end of his 'great adventure'. 'Next day I met my little wife again,' he ends his journal, 'and all the dangers and hardships of Gallipoli were washed away, forgotten in that moment.'

AT SEA

AT SEA

8 Battle of Jutland Survivor

'I believe that they are out, and we have got a grand time in front of us', was how Petty Officer Ernest Francis, a gunner's mate aboard the battlecruiser *Queen Mary*, heard from his gunnery officer on the morning of 31 May 1916 that the German High Seas Fleet might be in the offing and that the British Grand Fleet might soon be engaging it in a sea battle to rate with Trafalgar.

The gunnery officer was right. Some five hours later the first salvoes of the battle of Jutland roared out. But for the 1,000 officers and men of the *Queen Mary* that 'grand time' was to be short-lived. Less than forty minutes later Francis was among a handful of survivors struggling for life in an oil-coated sea. The great ironclad that had for long been his home had blown up and sunk almost without trace.

The battle of Jutland is one of the most written-about and argued-about naval engagements in British history and the account Francis wrote about his brief participation adds little of factual significance. But as a human document, written by a sailor 'much handier behind a pair of 13.5 inch turret guns than a pen', it gives some idea of what it felt to be in the thick of a great sea battle: one moment a tiny cog in a seemingly impregnable complex of floating machinery, the next a man alone fighting the sea.

Francis wrote his account in the form of a letter to the senior surviving officer of the *Queen Mary*, Midshipman Van der Byl,

shortly after recovering from his ordeal, and brief excerpts from it have been used in one or two of the many books about the battle of Jutland. A copy of it was sent to the *Sunday Times* by a retired admiral who had found it in his possession, and it is here for the first time reproduced in full.

The account starts on 30 May when, following news that the German High Seas Fleet was putting to sea, the Grand Fleet was about to sail out from its bases at Scapa Flow, Cromarty and Rosyth, to confront it. The *Queen Mary*, with an armament of eight 13.5 inch guns, sixteen 4 inch guns, and two 21 inch torpedo tubes, was one of the six battlecruisers of the Battlecruiser Fleet under Admiral Beatty, which was to bear the brunt of the early fighting.

'My first impression starts from the day we went to sea. I had a class under instructions in field training in the starboard waist abreast "Q" turret during the forenoon, when the Engineer Writer came along, and as he passed he whispered "Short Notice". Shortly afterwards I noticed that all ships were getting up steam for all they were worth. Mr Sturt, our Chief Gunner, came along and said "Francis, if I were you I should get the aiming and Dotter apparatus unrigged and stowed away, as we are under very short notice, and may be off at any time".

'Well I did not take very much notice of this because I had to do this many times before and then nothing had turned up and I have had to rig it all up again, an operation which took nearly half a day in order to adjust the apparatus properly. It made one rather careful unless one was nearly certain we were going to sea. What finally decided me was our fine gunnery officer, who came along and said "All the gear unrigged, Francis?" I said "Not yet, sir", to which he replied: "I should get on with it if I were you, we may be on the move any moment." That decided me and I took the class and unrigged the two 4 inch Aiming teachers, the two 4 inch Dotters and the 13.5 inch Dotter on "X" turret.

'By this time it was 12 o'clock dinner time, and I went to

dinner. Whilst there Mr Sturt came along and wanted me to go round my own turret magazine and see whether top cases had their lashings on, and asked me to tell the other gunner's mates to go round their turrets, which I did. After seeing to my own turret I went to the 4 inch magazines, shellrooms and ready use magazine to see if everything was clear, this being my ordinary routine when under short notice, not that I had any special idea that we were going to sea, but when I came on deck afterwards and found we were under way I felt quite pleased to think that everything was nicely squared off and unrigged.

'After this it was just ordinary routine, ie both batteries were well looked to, ammunition placed, watch set in the foremost battery, and we just talked as usual. Of course the usual buzzes were started, but I know that nobody had any idea we were on a big errand. The night of the 30th went off very quietly, with no spasms of any description except that the order was passed to the gunner's mates that a very special watch was to be kept in the batteries during the night.

'Between 10 and 11 am on the 31st I met the Gunnery Officer and he said "Francis, I want to see all the gunner's mates in my cabin now" so off I went to get hold of the other three, and we all went in. Mr Llewellyn said, "Now, look here, I sent for you to ask each one to go to his turret and examine from top to bottom to see that everything is up to date. I know that everything is all right but I want you to do this and come and make your reports afterwards. My reason for doing this is that I believe that they are out, and we have a grand time in front of us".

'Well we had heard this before so many times that I suppose we must have smiled or done something to show that we didn't think much of it, because he said to Harrison, our Chief Gunner's Mate, "Don't you believe it, Harrison?" to which Harrison replied, "Well, sir, seeing is believing, and if they have really come out, I will take back one or two of the remarks I have made about them at different times."

'So off we went and had a good overhaul. In the case of "X" turret I knew before I went round that I should find everything all right because Lt Ewert was wrapped up in his turret, and many an hour have I spent with him, explaining the working of the various machinery. His one aim was efficiency, if at any time a new man came into the turret he would worry about him until I reported to him that the new man knew his job and could be trusted to fill up any casualties in action. I shall have more to say of this smart young officer later on.

'I went over "X" turret from top to bottom, and I really felt quite pleased with everything. It was complete down to spare lengths of flexible piping, urinal buckets, biscuits and corned beef, drinking water and plenty of first aid dressings. I went to the Commander (G) and made my report. He thanked me, and repeated again that he thought they were out. I said: "I sincerely hope they are, Sir, as it is uphill work keeping the men up to the idea of meeting them again. If we can only manage to get a few salvoes into our old opponents the German Battle Cruisers, it will put new life into the crowd." The conversation then drifted back to the Heligoland Bight scrap, and he said: "If we do have a smash, I hope it will be your luck to repeat your previous performance." He was referring to the damage my guns did in the third round in local control. I quite agreed with him, as I hoped for such luck again.

'The remainder of the gunner's mates made their reports I know, and made quite a joke about "Old Guns" trying to make us think they were out. At any rate, we didn't think much about it, but went to dinner and after dinner we went down to the diving room, which belonged to the gunner's mates and made our arrangements for a sleep. I had the First Dog in the battery so I made arrangements with the gunner's mate on watch to send down and let me know when it was 3.30 pm. We lay down and had quite a comfortable sleep, having nothing on our minds to keep us awake; the only thing we were sure about was a ship full of coal waiting to have about 2,000 tons taken out of her.

'At about 3.30 pm an able seaman came down and said "Petty Officer Francis, it is nearly 7 bells." I thanked him and said "Anything doing up on top?" He said, "No". I got up and took off my jumper and had a wash, and just as I finished I heard in the distance the bugle sound of "Action". I was so surprised that I could hardly believe my ears, but the rush of feet by the door forced it upon me. I called to Harrison and P.O. Clarke and told them they had sounded off "Action". Poor old Harrison said "What's the matter with you, can't you sleep?" but before I could answer another bugle sounded off and no more words were necessary.

'It was a scramble to get away. Harrison said "Good luck, Ernie, the TS will back you up". I said "Righto Governor" and we were gone. I took the first hatchway up, as doors were closing, and came up the foremost 4 inch battery, starboard side, and raced for "X" turret. When I got there everyone was inside. I yelled out "Turrets crew number". They were correct from top to bottom and I reported to Lt Ewert. He said "Test Loading Gear, but for goodness sake don't let them get too rash. I wouldn't miss one round in this smash for worlds".

'The loading gear and machinery were tested, and afterwards came the order to load all cages. As soon as they were loaded it was reported to the T.S. and then came the order to load. The guns were loaded and brought to the half cock and reported, and then came the order to bring the right gun to the ready. Director Laying and Firing. Shortly after this, the first salvo was fired, and we started on the great game. I had no means of telling what the time was, and if I had, I probably should not have looked, because getting a Turret starting is an anxious rushing time for a Captain of a Turret. Once started it is easy to keep going. Taking everything into consideration, I put it as about 3.45 pm or 3.55 pm, that's as near as I can go.'

[The British battlecruisers opened fire at 3.48 pm. The *Queen Mary* blew up at 4.26 pm.]

'The guns crew were absolutely perfect, inclined to be a little slow in loading, but I gave them a yell and pointed out to them that I wanted a steady stride. After that everything went like clockwork until both rammers gave out, my gun going first. This was caused by number 3 opening the breech before the gun had run out after firing: the carrier arm must have hit the rammer head and slightly metal bound it. I dropped the elevating wheel, got hold of a steel bar, forced the end in behind the rammer head, at the same time putting the lever to "Run out". Out went the rammer, and I rushed it back again, and it all went gay again; then the lever was over at the right gun and both rammers were again in working order.

'I was pleased to get them both going, as it would have been such a damper on the crew if we had to go into hand loading. My number 3 said "PO Francis, can you see what we are up against?" Well I had been anxious to have a look round, but could not spare the time, but as soon as my gun had fired and while the loading was being completed, I had a look through the periscopes, and it seemed to me that there were hundreds of masts and funnels. I dropped back into my seat and laid my gun by pointer, being in director firing, and while the loading was being completed again, I told them there were a few battle cruisers out, not wishing to put a damper on them in any way; not that I think it would have done so, as they were all splendid fellows and backed me up magnificently.

'Up till now I had not noticed any noise, such as being struck by a shell, but afterwards there was a heavy blow, struck, I should imagine, in the after 4 inch battery, and a lot of dust and pieces flying around on the top of "X" turret. My attention was called by the turret trainer, AB Long, who reported the front glass of his periscope blocked up. This was not very important because we were in director training, but some one in rear heard him report his glass foul and without orders dashed on top and cleared it. He must have been smashed up as he did it, for he fell in front of the periscope and then apparently fell on to the turret. I wish I knew his name, poor chap, but it's no use guessing.

'Another shock was felt shortly after this, but it did not affect the turret, so no notice was taken. Then the T.S. reported to Lt Ewert that the third ship of the line was dropping out. First blood to *Queen Mary*. The shout they gave was good to hear. I could not resist giving a quick look at her, at their request, and I found that the third ship of the line was going down by the bows. I felt the turret travel a bit faster than she had been moving, and surmised we must have shifted on to the fourth ship of the line; being in director firing, no orders were required for training.

'I looked again and found the third ship of the line was gone, so I turned to the spare gun layer, PO Killick, who was recording the number of rounds fired, and he said thirty some odd figures, I didn't catch the exact number. A few more rounds were fired when I took another look through my telescope and there was quite a fair distance between the second ship and what I believed was the fourth ship, due I think to third ship going under. Flames were belching from what I took to be the fourth ship of the line, then came the big explosion which shook us a bit, and on looking at the pressure gauge I saw the pressure had failed. Immediately after that came, what I term, the big smash, and I was dangling in the air on a bowline, which saved me from being thrown down on the floor of the turret. These bowlines were an idea I brought into my turret and each man in the gunhouse was supplied with one, and as far as I noticed the men who had them on were not injured in the big smash. No. 2 and 3 of the left gun slipped down under the gun and the gun appeared to me to have fallen through its trunnions and smashed up these two numbers.

'Everything in the ship went as quiet as a church, the floor of the turret was bulged up and the guns were absolutely useless.

I must mention here that there was not a sign of excitement. One man turned to me and said "What do you think has happened?" I said, "Steady, every one, I will speak to Mr Ewert". I went back to the Cabinet and said, "What do you think has happened, Sir?" He said, "God knows!" "Well, Sir," I said, "It's no use keeping them all down here. Why not send them up on the 4 inch guns, and give them a chance to fight it out? As soon as the Germans find we are out of action they will concentrate on us and we shall all be going sky high." He said, "Yes, good idea, just see if the 4 inch guns aft are still standing."

'I put my head through the hole in the roof of the turret and nearly fell through again. The after 4 inch battery was smashed out of all recognition, and then I noticed that the ship had got an awful list to port. I dropped back again into the turret and told Lt Ewert the state of affairs. He said, "Francis, we can do no more than give them a chance, clear the turret."

' "Clear the turret," I said, and out they went. PO Stares was the last I saw coming up from the Working Chamber, and I asked him whether he had passed the order to the Magazine and Shell Room, and he told me it was no use as the water was right up to the trunk leading to the shell room, so the bottom of the ship must have been torn out of her. Then I said, "Why didn't you come up?" He simply said, "There was no order to leave the turret."

'I went through the cabinet and out on top and Lt Ewert was following me; suddenly he stopped and went back into the turret. I believe he went back because he thought someone was inside. I cannot say enough for Lt Ewert, nothing I can say would do him justice. He came out of the turret cabinet twice and yelled something to encourage the guns crew, and yelled out to me "All right, Francis". He was grand, and I would like to publish this account to the World. It makes me feel sore hearted when I think of Lt Ewert and that fine crowd who were with me in the turret.

'I can only write about the behaviour of my own turret's crew, but I am confident knowing the *Queen Mary* as I did, that the highest traditions of the Service were upheld by the remainder of the Ship's Company, from the Captain to the smallest boy. Everyone was so keen on being in a big smash, and each member of the Ship's Company knew he was one of the small cog wheels of a great machine. It was part of a man's training as laid down by our fine Gunnery Commander, Mr Llewellyn, and due to his untiring efforts to make the *Queen Mary* the splendid fighting unit I knew her to be.'

In the bitter opening duel of the battle of Jutland, of which Francis in his gun turret had actually witnessed so very little, the German battlecruisers under Admiral Franz von Hipper got the better of their British opposite numbers, scoring 40 hits against 10. The *Lion* (Admiral Beatty's flagship), *Tiger* and *Princess Royal* were all hit, and, shortly before the *Queen Mary* went down, another single salvo from a German battlecruiser blew up *Indefatigable*, all but two of her 1,000 officers and men losing their lives.

A distant impression, from the decks of an enemy ship, of the sinking of the *Queen Mary* was given by a German naval officer, Commander von Hase. 'The enemy was shooting superbly. Twice the *Derfflinger* came under their infernal hail and each time she was hit. But the *Queen Mary* was having a bad time; engaged by the *Seydlitz* as well as by the *Derfflinger*, she met her doom at 1626. A vivid red flame shot up from her forepart; then came an explosion forward which was followed by a much heavier explosion amidships. Immediately afterwards she blew up with a terrific explosion, the masts collapsing inwards and the smoke hiding everything.' Francis now goes on to describe how he came to be one of the handful to survive by jumping overboard just before that final 'smash'.

'I was half way down the ladder at the back of the turret when Lt Ewert went back. The ship had an awful list to port by this time, so much so that men getting off the ladder, went sliding down to port. I got to the bottom rung of the ladder and could not, by my own efforts, reach the stanchions lying on the deck from the ship's side, starboard side. I knew if I let go I should go sliding down to port like some of the others must have done, and probably got smashed up sliding down. Two of my turret's crew, seeing my difficulty, came to my assistance. They were AB Long, Turret Trainer, and AB Lane, left gun No 4. Lane held Long at full length from the ship's side and I dropped from the ladder, caught Long's legs and so gained the starboard side. These two men had no thought for their own safety; they knew I wanted assistance and that was good enough for them. They were both worth a VC twice over.

'When I got to the ship's side, there seemed to be quite a fair crowd, and they didn't appear to be very anxious to take to the water. I called out to them "Come on you chaps, who's coming for a swim?" Someone answered "She will float for a long time yet", but something, I don't pretend to know what it was, seemed to be urging me to get away, so I clambered over the slimy bilge keel and fell off into the water, followed I should think by about five more men. I struck away from the ship as hard as I could and must have covered nearly fifty yards when there was a big smash, and stopping and looking round, the air seemed to be full of fragments and flying pieces.

'A large piece seemed to be right above my head, and acting on impulse, I dipped under to avoid being struck, and stayed under as long as I could, and then came to the top again, and coming behind me I heard a rush of water, which looked very like surf breaking on a beach and I realised it was the suction or backwash from the ship which had just gone. I hardly had time to fill my lungs with air when it was on me. I felt it was no use struggling against it, so I let myself go for a moment or two, then I struck out, but I felt it was a losing game and remarked to myself "What's the use of you struggling, you're done", and I actually ceased my efforts to reach the top, when a small voice seemed to say "Dig out".

'I started afresh, and something bumped against me. I grasped it and afterwards found it was a large hammock, but I felt I was getting very weak and roused myself sufficiently to look around for something more substantial to support me. Floating right in front of me was what I believe to be the centre bulk of our Pattern 4 target. I managed to push myself on the hammock close to the timber and grasped a piece of rope hanging over the side. My next difficulty was to get on top and with a small amount of exertion I kept on. I managed to reeve my arms through a strop and I must have become unconscious.

'When I came to my senses again I was half way off the spar but I managed to get back again. I was very sick and seemed to be full of oil fuel. My eyes were blocked up completely with it and I could not see. I suppose the oil had got a bit crusted and dry. I managed by turning back the sleeve of my jersey, which was thick with oil, to expose a part of the sleeve of my flannel, and thus managed to get the thick oil off my face and eyes, which were aching awfully. Then I looked and I believed I was the only one left of that fine Ship's Company. What had really happened was the *Laurel* had come and picked up the remainder and not seeing me got away out of the zone of fire, so how long I was in the water I do not know. I was miserably cold, but not without hope of being picked up, as it seemed to me that I had only to keep quiet and a ship would come for me.

'After what seemed ages to me, some destroyers came racing along, and I got up on the spar, steadied myself for the moment, and waved my arms. The *Petard*, one of our big destroyers, saw me and came over, but when I got on the spar to wave to them, the swell rolled the spar over and I rolled off. I was nearly exhausted again getting back. The destroyer came up and a line was thrown to me, which, needless to say, I grabbed hold of for all I was worth, and was quickly hauled up on to the deck of the destroyer. The first words I heard spoken were "Are you English or German?"'

'I remember no more until I came to and found I was lying on what appeared to be a leather settee and someone was telling me I was all right and not to struggle. I could not see the faces around me, so concluded I was blind, but did not feel that it mattered so much; my thoughts flew to the fine crowd who had gone under.

'I was given some spirits of some sort and then I must have gone to sleep. Someone came over to me and said "Don't get excited if you hear any shooting, we are just going to carry out an attack on a big German". I wasn't in a fit state to worry much about attacks on Germans. My eyes were very painful, and I must have said something about them, for I believe a young doctor came down to bathe them, when suddenly there was a big smash, and I was told afterwards that a shell came through, killed the doctor and eight men and I never received a scratch. I couldn't see, and being a gunnery man, I took the big smash to be a 4 inch gun being fired. I had no idea it was a German shell.

'I must have gone to sleep again, when I was awakened by some of the chaps who were taking me down to the petty officers' quarters, as by this time they had found out I was a gunner's mate. I believe in the first place I told them I was a stoker. Nothing happened after this of any importance, only I was in awful agony with my eyes. I was told that we were steaming at greatly reduced speed to Rosyth, and arrived as near as I can guess, about midnight on the first of June.

'The Hospital Boat came over, and I was very quickly taken to Queensferry Hospital, where I was soon made nice and comfortable in bed, feeling that my troubles were over, and thanking God, who, I feel, was very near me on that great day and pulled me through.

'I fell asleep, and woke up to find the doctor waiting to clean my eyes. He would not disturb me before. After my eyes had been cleaned and seen to, I felt much relieved. The doctor told me to keep the bandage on and my eyes would be all right again soon. I left the hospital on Monday, having previously asked the Fleet Surgeon to let me go south for two days running. I felt the groans of the burnt and wounded would have driven me mad. He told me if I could get some clothes I could go. I met a wardmaster who I had known some years before and he fitted me out with some clothes, gathered from the hospital staff, and made me quite presentable.

'I left Edinburgh by the midnight train and on arrival in London went to the Union Jack Club, where I had a good breakfast, and after a wash and a shave went to see Captain (now Rear Admiral) Hall, by appointment, but he was called away and I was very disappointed at not seeing him. He commissioned the *Queen Mary* with Commander James and started a routine that made her the smartest and most comfortable ship afloat.

'I left London and arrived at the Royal Naval Barracks, Portsmouth, where I reported myself and was allowed to go home. The next day I was given some clothes, and after seeing the doctor, who advised me what to do about my eyes, very kindly allowed me to go home on fourteen days leave.

'When I returned off leave I was given a kit of clothes and sent to Whale Island (my depot) being a gunner's mate. When I saw the doctor, he said, "Your nerves are gone, you want a rest", and sent me home for another fourteen days leave. When I returned off leave I was feeling much better and my eyes were nearly well again. At the time of writing they are all right, but they tire very quickly, and I am now working with the Store Gunner of Whale Island.

'To finish my account, I will say that I believe the cause of the ship being blown up was a shell striking "B" turret working chamber, and igniting the shells stowed there in the ready racks, and the flash must have passed into the magazine, and that was the finish.'

AT HOME

9　*Front Line, Home Front*

'This being the greatest war the World has ever known, it may be of some interest in years to come, if we survive, to have a few notes of local events in this little Frontier Coast Town of Southwold lying at this moment within 80 miles of the front in Belgium and not more than 250 from the great War Harbours of Germany.'

Thus Mr Ernest Read Cooper, solicitor and Town Clerk of Southwold, prefaces, in a bold sloping hand, the journal he wrote up after the war from the diary he had kept whenever he could snatch time from his manifold activities. At the outbreak of war he had been Town Clerk for the past nineteen years, and was also Clerk to the Magistrates, Manager of the Harbour, Secretary of the Ferry Company, Secretary of the Lifeboats, Captain of the Fire Brigade, and Secretary of the Waterworks. In May 1916 he lists some of his additional wartime appointments: Commandant of the Volunteers, Clerk to the Tribunal, Secretary of the Canadians' Fund, Sub-Commander of Pilotage, Deputy Lloyds' Agent, 'besides smaller jobs'.

Cooper was, indeed, something of a Pooh Bah in this picturesque old Suffolk resort, but there is more dry humour than pomposity in his delightful portrayal of life on the Home Front. There is no lack of the growsing that helps keep civilians happy in wartime—the price of food and its increasing scarcity,

187

the behaviour of troops billeted on the town, the weather, some of which he even blames on artillery barrages on the Western Front. But it is evident that Southwold regarded itself as a special case, more vulnerable to the Germans than almost anywhere in England. It was on the direct path of Zeppelins crossing the North Sea to bomb London and other targets in south-east England. Far more, it was at the mercy of German naval raiders and invading troops. The fear of invasion persisted up to the last month of the war, when new pill boxes were being proposed to strengthen the coastal defences.

But even though the German menace was felt to be close, the journal, written as it is by a public servant very much at the centre of things, revealingly hints at the impassable gulf that existed between the Home Front and the trenches. Cooper's devoted championing of the Volunteers—recruiting meetings, inspections, drills—has a faintly comic air about it now, shades of a later Dad's Army. The real war was elsewhere. On still nights in Southwold they could sometimes hear the dull boom of the guns in Flanders. It came from another, undreamed-of world.

The journal starts on 28 July 1914.

'My wife and I went on board our yacht *Louie* this day having let our house for a month and altho' there was war in the air on the continent it was not supposed that we should be drawn in, but on the second night on board, about 1.30 am on the 30 Inst, we were awakened by Noel hammering on deck and shouting, he said the Postmaster had called him up and sent him down with two important telegrams. I was sleepy and wanted to discuss the matter but he was very cross at being turned out and shoved the telegrams thro' the skylight and scooted. They turned out to be telegrams from the Board of Trade that no lights were to be extinguished nor buoys removed without the concurrence of the Admiralty, one was addressed to me as Town Clerk and the other as Manager of the Harbour.

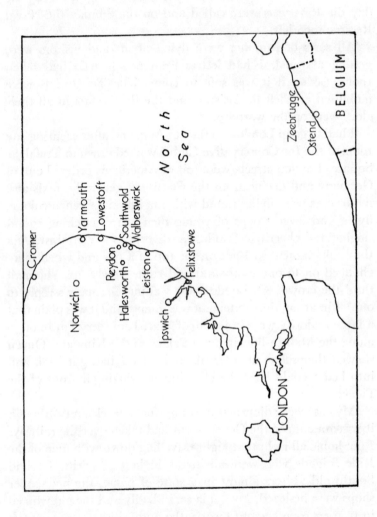

Sissie said at once, that means War with Germany, and when we went up to the Town in the morning we found that all the Coastguard had been taken away during the night, during the day the Reservists were called and on the Sunday the Naval Reserve men left.

'All sorts of rumours were flying about and visitors were getting alarmed. I had letters from people who had taken rooms asking if it was safe to come. The Territorials were mobilised and left for Leiston and the Boy Scouts in all their glory were on the warpath.

'I had to go to London on the 4th Aug. and after securing my room at the Jnr Conservative Club I walked down to Trafalgar Square. London streets were full of Americans ordered out of Germany and fleeing from the Continent generally, taxis and motor cars were flying round with English and French colours flying and large troops of young men were marching round singing and cheering. Traffic was diverted to Westminster via the Embankment so I got on the top of a bus and when there changed on to one eastbound and came slowly up Whitehall thro' the crowd. All London was waiting Germany's reply to our Ultimatum, the excitement was intense and it was plain that a large majority were in favour of War. I am sorry I did not go along the Mall to Buckingham Palace as the King and Queen shewed themselves at intervals and after I had got back and into bed I could hear the cheering and singing in front of the Palace.

'My case was adjourned next day for a week and although it was announced the Government had taken over the railways I got home all right that night travelling down with men of the Rifle Brigade who were all in the highest of spirits. I found Southwold visitors almost in a state of panic, the newspaper shops were besieged, spymania set in badly and the old women in trousers soon began to worry the authorities.

'We lived on board the yacht all the month, several yachts were in the Harbour at the time of the Declaration, some got away at once, other men laid theirs up and went off for a time, Lewis could not look after us properly as he was "all of a flutter" and each morning when he knocked on the cabin door he told us all the latest news. Very soon came the news of HMS *Amphion* and the mines and her smashed boat was washed ashore here —then some mine sweepers appeared and began sweeping a channel for the coasters, one of their first acts was to catch the warp of Bob Harris' trawl boat and sink it nearly drowning him . . .

'We had sent Judith and the nurse to lodge at Wenhaston while the house was let and used to run up the river in the motor boat to see them, Nurse amused me by saying, "Since the War's been on I always sleep with my window fastened". Things seemed so unsafe outside that we never let go our moorings and directly our house was vacant we moved in and laid the yacht up. The Rev Pawley Smith was there in his boat and had his gardener as steward, one day he asked Fred if there was any news and the gardener solemnly replied, "Well sir they do say up in the town as them Jarmans have took Barlin".

'A week or two later I was appointed Joint Hon. Secretary of the local Branch of the East Suffolk War Relief Fund and we raised over £600 in Southwold & District, in connection with this I organised a recruiting meeting in the Market Place which resulted in over sixty recruits joining including two of my own clerks, Peck and Moore (I am glad to add both of these returned safely in 1919 after over four years service abroad) . . . The new recruits left on 7 Sept and they mustered in the Market Place and we had the band and crowds to the station to see them off. A few days after as one of the National Reserve I accompanied those who had been called up down to the station and each time I saw old Col. Sergeant Mackenzie looking out of his window watching and I wondered if he thought of the days when he was at the Crimea with the Scots Guards. (He died 2 Feb. 1915 aged 86, I arranged for the Funeral and the

25th Londons furnished the Firing Party, his old Regt sent
a wreath) . . .

'*31 Oct.* A troop of Lincolnshire Yeomanry came in and I
let them into the Waterworks Enclosure on the Common
where they made a most horrible mess, damaged the fence,
gave my men a lot of trouble and then refused to pay the modest
sum of 10/- asked for water and accommodation of forty-four
horses for two nights . . .

'We hardly realised what War really meant until the 15 Oct.
when the Ostend smack *Anna Williams 028* arrived in the
Harbour with Belgian Refugees and saw numbers of other
smacks making for Lowestoft. I boarded her with a pilot at the
Harbour mouth and found her crowded with men women and
children from seventy years to an infant, who had fled just as
they were with pitiful little bundles and boxes, leaving everything else to the Germans who were reported just outside
Ostend. These people were well looked after by the Southwold
folks but were ordered to London and left next day in a special
motor bus for Halesworth where they joined the Lowestoft
refugees about 1,000 in number. There was great excitement
about these poor people and we thought it might be our fate
later . . .

'One of the results of the War was that owners of big Shoots
could not get guns and I had more shooting this Season than
ever before, shooting with Ewen at Reydon, at Hensham,
Dunwich, Sotterley and Brampton besides my own little shoot
at Reydon and had to refuse a number of days. I was shooting
with Colman at Wrentham and on returning home heard of the
attempted bombardment of Yarmouth and Lowestoft by
German men of war. I had been doing a little Insurance at
Lloyds against War Risks and this caused the premium to jump
from 5/- to 10/-, I had luckily covered my own little home
for £1,500 at 5/-. . . .

'*25 Nov.* The Council had a special meeting as to arrangements in case of invasion and after much talk I was to confer

with the Military Authorities. Next day the Mayor, myself and
the Parish Officer of Special Constables and others went to
Walberswick and met Gen. Herbert in command of this district
and various others and so far as I could gather his idea was that
we should do nothing but go quietly about our business and
remain within in case of a landing or bombardment, he said he
could not get any quantity of troops to Southwold under four
or five hours but that an Emergency Committee was being
formed for the District who would issue instructions. I assisted at
the swearing in of some thirty special constables for Southwold
and altho' I was not of that body I believe they made elaborate
and probably impracticable schemes for operations in case
of invasion. I was asked for a list of all vessels laid up in the
Harbour and of the Firearms in my possession and printed
instructions were issued as to the removal of the civil population . . .

'As things were looking lively in the North Sea and we were
promised more raids I packed up my silver in a box and my
sister Clara Stanford took it one day in her car to Halesworth
and our baby not having been well I thought a change of air
would be best for her and the wife so we arranged for them to
go to Grannie at Sutton Surrey as soon as she was well enough
and on the 11th Dec. they departed, we discharged the maids
and closed the house. I went to the Boarding house next door and
lived a wandering life between the two houses. A few days after
occurred the bombardment of Scarbro and Hartlepool and
up went the War Risk prem. on the E. Coast to 30/-, people
began to get nervous and Visitors who were coming down
for Christmas cancelled their arrangements, the large St
Felix School for Girls broke up hurriedly on receipt of the
news and about 120 of them went down to the 2.20 train, there
was not room for all and a number had to ride in trucks seated
on boxes.

'I went to Sutton for Christmas returning alone on the 31st
to attend the Council meeting on the 1st Jany. when I found the

Duke of Westminster had come into the town with fifteen armoured cars and a number of men, it is rumoured they will remain here until they go to the Front about March.

1915
'Early in the New Year a fleet of steamdrifters arrived from Lowestoft and went up through the Railway Bridge to lay up for safety, some went nearly two miles up the river and I took the opportunity to get the *Louie* towed up by one of them and put her into Wolseys Creek in a safe and quiet berth . . . Great excitement was caused here by the news of the Air raid at Cromer and Yarmouth when Zeppelins dropped bombs there, I was at home and heard nothing but young Pipe of South Cove told me he was outside and heard the explosions at Yarmouth quite loud and all the pheasants started crowing in the woods altho' it was past 8 pm. After this very drastic regulations came out about lights, Orders were issued and the Special Constables made inspections from the Church Steeple and dropped on to offenders in all directions, but the minesweepers in the Bay were lit up like a town most nights . . .

'*22 Feb.* Sissie returned from Sutton with Judith and brought a new nurse, I met them at Halesworth with a car. I found baby much advanced, walking nicely and beginning to chatter. I was glad to get back home after three months in the boarding house but our new maid saw an aeroplane going over the house one evening so she packed up and when I went home to tea she was gone and I afterwards found she had walked home nearly to Beccles because she was afraid to stay in Southwold, we had great trouble in getting another . . .

'*13 March.* The 2/6th Batt. Royal Sussex Cyclists 670 strong came into the town and were billeted in empty houses, they caused us a lot of trouble by overcrowding the houses, damaging property and hatching infectious diseases, soon after they arrived the RNAS armoured cars departed having been about ten weeks and had a very good time. . . .

'*15/16 April*. This night there was an Air raid on Southwold Lowestoft etc, a Zeppelin passed over the town about 20 to 12 without dropping bombs and either this or another came back from London an hour later and we were awoke by a terrific explosion and immediately heard the loud whirring of the engines apparently over the west part of the Town, very quickly another explosion occurred and shook the whole place, we found the electric light had been cut off, Sissie hurried and got Judith and Nurse down into the Dining Room and having slipped on some clothes I followed with blankets rugs and cushions and made them comfortable in a corner, the horrid noise of the Zepp going on all the time and the soldiers running about, then we heard them firing at the airship and the bullets were dropping all about the Green but she seemed a long way off then. I dressed and went round to the Fire Station in case the engines should be wanted, two of my firemen came and we waited about some time. I heard three explosions away in the Lowestoft direction and soon after I got out the noise of the engines died away, there were a good many people in the streets and many houses had lights nearly everyone being awake and about. I went home and we made the best of it until past two when I went out again and found a clear starlight night and no sign nor sound of any more. The Sentry told me it was thought to be all over and so about 2.30 we got to bed again and woke very tired, I had been ill for ten days or so with laryngitis and flu and was feeling shaky.

'In the morning it appeared that bombs explosive or incendiary had been dropped at the Railway Station, where a truck was set on fire but soon put out, at Alder Car Works Henham Hall Reydonsmere and Lowestoft but little or no damage done. Many rumours and tales were flying about and streams of cars came in to see what had happened, with the Inhabitants it was business as usual but several visiting families packed up and left during the day, some by the 7.30 am. No doubt the raid was intended for London but petrol or darkness did not hold out so the Zepp had to turn back giving us a dose on the way. Many full accounts with Maps and Pictures were given in all the papers and immediately quoted in Germany, it seems they did not know where the bombs had been dropped until our papers told them and the accounts of later Raids were severely censored.

'Some amusing yarns went about, one of our fishermen was said to have looked out of his chamber window and seen it so close that he was going to knock it down with a stick only his wife said, "For God's sake don't do that, think of the children". Another of an old lady who was a bit of a midwife at Reydon outside whose garden a bomb was dropped making a hole 6 ft deep, she and the old man were in bed and she said, well if they do want me in a hurry they needn't have knocked all the windows in, and they picked glass out of the old boy's beard for a week after.

'About a fortnight after this the soldiers began to seriously fortify the Town, and as I heard from the Major that it was expected a raid would be made by sea to burn murder and destroy within sixty days I thought it time to take precautions so at the beginning of May we sent Nurse and baby up to Grannie as before and the week after Sissie and the maid went up and took over the house while the old Birds went to Wales for a three weeks cure. I was left alone with a housekeeper but went up and spent Whitsun at Sutton, a most welcome rest, for in place of constant night alarms, booming of distant guns at sea and the ever present proximity of War I found Sutton practically normal and one felt if not peace at any rate quite out of touch with war. I placed £150 and my Life and War risk Policies at the London Coy and Westminster Bk at Sutton so as to have something to go on with in case of destruction at Southwold and I afterwards increased this to £400 and sent most of my Securities up.'

Here Cooper relates at some length the steps that led up to the formation of a County Organisation of local corps of Volunteers, men not eligible for the other services. He was appointed Adjutant of the Lowestoft Battalion and writes, 'I found my old Volunteer experience very useful altho' after over 20 years the Drill was much altered'. He was kept very busy, with drills three nights a week, practice on a miniature range and fund-raising projects. He is bitter about the Government's attitude to the Volunteers. 'The work of organisation was difficult and tedious owing to the movement having been started the wrong end first and to the Government as usual discouraging the affair as much as possible. Their only contribution was a Brassard or Armlet of red with G.R. on it which was issued to each Member, all the rest of the Equipment, Rifles, Uniforms, Ammunition etc had to be found by the Corps, also Instructors and all expenses of formation and working'.

This period also saw the strengthening of Southwold's defences against an invasion, with a network of trenches and breastworks, barbed wire draping the face of the cliffs, wire fencing on the cliff edge, and the erection of a boom over the harbour entrance. It also saw the comings and goings of more troops, an event that provides a somewhat plaintive leitmotif to much of the journal.

'*1 July*. The 2/6 Royal Sussex marched out for Norwich and the Bedfords etc. known as the 68th Prov. Battn. took over from them. We had a detachment of the Sussex billeted behind our house and for the three months had a sentry outside my house day and night and after ten everyone was challenged, Hands Up Who goes there, so there was not much peace with night alarms and football on the Green by day, one day the football came through our window and covered the room with glass. The Bedfords mounted Guard in the Market Place at 6.30 and enlivened it with a most distracting performance with the Bugle band up and down past my office for half an hour. They also had a useful Brass Band which on several Sunday marches cheered the Volunteers with their martial strains . . .

'*26 Sept.* During the night the Montgomery Yeomanry arrived, there were three trains but most of the men and horses came by road from Dorchester being three days on the road, 500 horses were picketed on the Common and the men billeted on the householders, being supplied with rations, they were commanded by Lt. Col. Mytton and the Officers messed at the Grand. By arrangement with the Corporation we built wooden stables on the Common going down to the Station for 200 horses, about 80 were stabled in the Harbour Sheds and the rest in various stables about the Town. It was most interesting to watch the mounted parades on the Common and nice to hear trumpets sounding instead of the everlasting bugles but the officers who played polo and kept draghounds etc. did not hit it off with the 101st and Swertzee retaliated by getting the Quartering Committee of which he was a member to repudiate all the Yeomanry hiring arrangements as well as many others, this caused me no end of trouble and it was not until the Council petitioned the Sec. of War, the Prime Minister and the local MP that we eventually got some justice.'

On a number of occasions Cooper called out the Lifeboat to go to the aid of ships attacked by German submarines, sometimes accompanying it. As Fire Brigade Chief he was kept on his toes by Zeppelin scares. He was now a mainstay of the local Volunteers, the year's culminating point being a review of his men on Beccles Common when he rode on an old grey mare behind an approving General Sir Horace Smith Dorien. But even he was not above suspicion.

'One night in November we were all very much surprised to see the Lighthouse lit up and finding the Lighter Keeper had lit up on a telegram which might easily have been a bogey, I made enquiries and found it was by order of the Naval Base. Long afterwards I heard that that night the Yeomanry reported that signalling was going on from the back of my house and they surrounded it with an armed guard, but fortunately before breaking in they sent for Inspector Ruffles who came and had a look and explained to them it was the reflection from the Lighthouse. We were blissfully asleep and heard nothing of it.

1916
Zeppelins passing over, ships sunk at sea (by torpedoes, mines, gales), billeted troops even more of a nuisance, the Volunteers growing in strength and complexity—for Cooper there was no let-up. He even took on new responsibilities. These are but representative extracts from his account of a hectic year:

'I was appointed Clerk to the Tribunal under Lord Derby's scheme and the Military Service Acts and the first sitting took place on the 18th Feby. Not very many Southwold men applied but about 60 men from the 101st Prov. Battn. tried to get off but did not get much sympathy. The muddling weak unfair way in which the Radicals tried to keep the Voluntary System going and escape conscription was a miserable exhibition and all the work had to be done over and over again.

'The Canadian Govt. very liberally gave a cargo of wheat to relieve distress on the East Coast the proceeds of which formed the Canadian Relief Fund to help Lodging House Keepers to carry on. I attended a conference at Saxmundham and got £1,500 allocated for the Southwold District, a local Committee was formed to work it and as usual I was made Clerk. Further grants were made afterwards and during the next three years I had to administer this and distribute the Fund, this meant many Meetings and much work as well as some unpleasantness with unsuccessful candidates. This was however the salvation of many homes.

'*April*. The greatest strictness was shewn about lights, special constables and soldiers were very busy and people were prosecuted right and left. I had some very long Magistrates Sittings and smart fines were inflicted, the Victims were furious but it was obvious that our safety lay in absolute darkness. I never went out at night if I could help it and on moonless nights all were obliged to feel the way with a stick . . .

'*26 May*. Col. Hegan has resigned the command of the 101st and a Col. Sayle has succeeded him and has nearly driven us mad with bugle calls all over the town at all hours of the day and night. The Alarm blown for half an hour in the middle of the night is very disturbing and calculated to give the town away to the Terror that flies by night. The troops are constructing large dugouts on the beach at various points and it is said they will vacate the houses and go into them for the summer, or I say until the first high tide . . .

'*28 May*. Sunday morning I motored to Beccles, inspected the Volrs. and spoke to them on the subject of the new organization. I have been advocating that every man exempted from service in the Army should be passed into his local Volunteers for training and have recently had letters in the *East Anglian, Eastern Daily Press, Spectator* and *Halesworth Times*. This would be such an obvious advantage to the country that only the usual rotten political tactics hinder its adoption. The Anticonscriptionists die hard . . .

'*13 June*. Public service in memory of Lord Kitchener. The Authorities chose this wintry time to turn the Troops out into dugouts and tents and the doctors are looking for pneumonia. After the high tide there was a foot or two of water in all the beach dugouts . . .

'*2 Aug*. Another raid lasting here from Midnight to 3 am during which time many bombs were dropped all round with very heavy explosions. I went home and found all under the table. Judith took it very well, sleeping most of the time, but inquired, "Am I under the Diney table, am I asleep on the floor?" It was most harassing having three nights running and two attacks all round us but thanks to the absolute darkness and quiet in the Town we came out of it safely. The first night some of the visitors were a great nuisance, the women running about cackling and asking to be shewn the Zepps but they were so well snubbed that next night they were quieter . . .

'*4 Aug*. Second Anniversary of War, we attended in State an

Intercession Service altho' it seems to me God has very little to say to this War . . .

'*6 Aug*. I had moored the yacht right away up Wolsey creek to be well out of the way of the Soldiers and to be a refuge in case of need but going up today I found four West Riding Tommies spending a weekend on board. I cleared them off but altho' I wrote to their CO and claimed £2 for the damage done I got no satisfaction except that it stopped further damage. They had made her in a beastly state but it was rather amusing as we rowed up quietly and I jumped on board and looked down the skylight giving them quite a shock . . .

'*6 Sept*. The Vicar arranged a short service in the Market Place to pray for our men serving and it was my duty to read the names of the Southwold men, 346 in No., while the Vicar read the names of the 16 who have fallen so far, a long Roll of honour for so small a Town . . .

'*14 Sept*. We had a NW breeze and very high tide and next morning I found the beach dugouts had several feet of water in them . . .

'*23 Sept*. Our Wedding Day, when like the Gilpins we made a picnic at Chilvers Farm. Sissie and I went on the marshes with Lewis and I shot a brace of birds a rabbit and a snipe. Then nurse met us with Judith and we had tea on the hillside and so home at dusk, a lovely day, fine and still with promise of Air raids later and sure enough while having supper the Mayor came round with the warning and I went on duty very cross and tired and remained there until 3.30 am. (What a Wedding Day!) . . .

'*22 Oct*. Inspection of the Suffolk Volrs at Ipswich by Lord French . . . The Coy. Commandant kindly told Lord French the 3rd Battn. had more than doubled since I took it over and he afterwards wrote me a very congratulatory letter. I had made it my business to see all detachments before this great Inspection and had been out on this duty seven Sundays out of eight besides week nights . . .

'*17, 18* and *19 Nov.* Heavy east and south gales. Lots of planking, margarine, oil, stout and other cargo washed ashore also several bodies including a man with £25 10s in gold tied to his leg, no clue to his name. The Picket at Dingle broached a cask of Stout and drank it out of buckets . . .

'*25 Nov.* The Welsh Fusiliers came in from Bedford and next day the balance of the 101st Prov. Battn. marched out en route for Guildford after being here about fourteen months, too long for some as they were very troublesome and the officers slack and I should say very inexperienced in Coast Work. Personally I was glad to see the back of them, I could never get on with the Major and the Col. threatened me with arrest because I shut off the water which his men were stealing and wasting. It remains to be seen if the Welsh are going to be any better . . .

'*1 Dec.* To Ipswich to a meeting of the COs of Volr Battalions as to the new Army Council Instructions for Volunteer Training. I was able to tell Lord Cadogan that a German aeroplane had dropped bombs on his Sloane Street property the day before . . .

'*20 Dec.* My old Aunt Kate Cooper died aged 85 and was buried at Blybro' in a howling gale. I caught a cold superintending the opening of the Family Vault on the 23rd, Judith was taken very ill the same night so that we had a miserable Christmas and all plans were capsized.'

1917

The major excitement of another hectic year, was the brief bombardment of Southwold by German light-draft naval vessels during a freezing gale on the night of 25 January. Two starshells with parachute lights illuminated the town while sixty-eight shells were fired. Although only five of the shells hit the town, the rest falling inland or in the sea, damage was trifling and no one was hurt, Cooper described the long-feared bombardment at greater length than any other happening during the war. The importance attached to this portent of possible perils to come is evident from these extracts:

'*25 Jan.* I went up just before 2.0 so as to be in Bed before the light went off and had been in bed about ten minutes when there was a double explosion followed almost directly by another very loud and close like the Lifeboat Gun. I jumped out of bed but in a moment came crashes of gunfire, very fast and loud and I told the Missis to hurry and get the baby down as the Germans were upon us. I ran down to get a light and make up the bomb-proof table with a terrific and rapid fire going on all the time. Before we had got things right the firing ceased just as abruptly as it began and we heard no more, it lasted five minutes from 11.5 to 11.10 and in that little time they put sixty-eight shells and two starshells into and over us. As soon as I could dress and rig up warmly for such a bitter midnight gale I turned out to the Fire Station but found no one there and very few people about . . .

'The double explosion we first heard were the starshells which fell one at Easton and the other on Chilvers Farm and lit up the whole Town. I saw one of the parachutes when it was brought in. I rather expect they then ranged on the Water Tower and the Light House as one or two shells passed between Southwold House and Blois' House, damaged Iona Cottage considerably, passed through the roof of Summer House, struck the ground on Skilmans Hill, ricochetted over the road and struck the Common on the rise and fell spent between the Oaktrees and the Watertower . . .

'Iona Cottages was widely damaged by splinters of shrapnel and I saw six holes in one ceiling, two went through the bed and down into the room below. Nearly every room was damaged except the one in which the Prestwidges were sleeping so again Providence was on our side and the Kaiser's old German God let him down once more. Probably we have to thank the heavy sea and darkness for the wild shooting together with the ever present fear of the British Navy . . .

'So far as I saw the townspeople behaved extremely well,

there was no panic, the Special Constables were out but very few others and most folks seem to have gone to bed again quietly. Some of the papers called it a comic bombardment and a silly raid just as they did about the early Zeppelin raids but to those who were in it there was nothing comic or silly but a very present danger. To speak as the papers do is to encourage the Germans to come again and make a job of it as they easily could under favourable conditions. So far as I know there was no reply from the shore and I don't know that we have any guns which would have been of use if there had been time . . .

'Sissie was walking along the shore a few days after and saw a cap floating on the breakers and some men trying to get it. She sent in my Retriever "Gunner" who brought ashore a German Sailor's cap with O.Z. on it and this and the shells are all they left behind them. My sister at Halesworth heard the bombardment and saw the shells bursting, she got up and made a fire in case we should have to leave Southwold but it is most apparent to me now that in a case of this sort there is no time to do much but take cover and you must just grin and bear it.'

Another highlight of the year was the shooting down of a Zeppelin on 16 June.

'Shortly after 12 there was a tremendous crash which shook the whole Town. Going in I found that my wife (poor wretch as Pepys says) had got Judith down ready to go into the cellar altho' the unlucky kiddie had a bad cough . . . About 3 am the gunfire broke out again heavily and standing on the Green in front of my house I saw shells bursting in the sky and I called the Missis out to see. Then the gunfire ceased suddenly and at 3.30 there was a big burst of flame in the sky over South-wold House and we saw it was a Zeppelin alight. She soon broke in two and then began to descend in a wavy line, roaring flames at the head and a long tail of sparks and smoke far up behind. She came down very slowly at first and I had a good view with my glasses, I think quite 3 to 4 minutes. When nearer the ground she came down faster and I plainly saw her strike the earth and rebound with a great flare of light.

'It was a great sight and the people who were out all cheered and those who were in bed came running out in their night dresses. It was then quite day and the Green was alive with people. Unfortunately for Judith she slept quietly thro' this historic occasion which possibly was as well . . . The Capt of the Zepp and two men landed alive which seems almost incredible but we hear one died afterwards. I think 17 were killed . . .'

The biggest political event of the year caused little stir in Southwold.

'It was surprising what a little difference the Political Crisis and change of Govt. made here. There was no excitement nor discontent as far as I could see but a generally expressed relief that we had at last got rid of old Asquith and his Wait and See Ministry. But for his party there would have been no war for some years and certainly if they had been at all competent it might have been over by now and we should not have had the food shortage which is now threatening us.'

Food and other shortages become a recurrent theme.

'Food is getting dear and some things almost improcurable, eggs 4½ butter 2/4 and most people including us are using margarine. A large quantity of this was washed ashore from a torpedoed Dutchman and I expect a lot of it took the place of butter for the poor people. My dog brought me several half pounds . . .

'There was a Win the War Meeting at Reydon School and I spoke on the need for economy, use of waste land and everyone doing something. I dwelt upon the need to wear up all old clothes and destroy nothing and an old man at the back called out, "Ha' yew got an oud suit or tew, Master, cos I'll wear 'em for you" which caused much laughter . . .

'We are running a Food Control Committee issuing Sugar Cards etc. but fixed prices promise to make things much scarcer and all the tradespeople seem to be on the make. I hardly ever see a bit of bacon, marmalade, jam, paraffin and matches are all difficult to get and very dear. I expect to have at least 5 cwt of potatoes from the garden I am cultivating with Meadows so that I should avoid starvation whatever happens if they don't go bad . . .'

Even the weather is blamed on the war.

'*31 July*. The British offensive at Ypres started and very heavy and continuous firing was audible. It produced as usual a torrential fall of rain and during the week ending the 4th Aug. at 9 am we had 4.66 inches of rain, the greatest weekly fall recorded so far. In spite of what the Scientific johnnies say our experience on this coast during the war satisfied me that this frenzy of heavy gun fire almost always results in deluges of rain . . .'

On 13 November Cooper saw his wife and daughter off on the train from London to Southbourne for the winter.

'I returned myself by 7 train to South Green House and a Housekeeper, a lone lorn crittur as Mrs Gummidge would have said. I am taking advantage of the first evening alone to write up this Log. After over three years of War's Alarms on the East Coast and the continued delicacy of the child I thought it well they should get away out of Air raids and far from Gunfire and exploding mines. Very few here are in their usual health, I have probably lost about two stones in weight owing to worry and rations but do not feel much the worse for it at present altho' I dread another cold winter like last . . .

'*15 Dec*. Shut up the house and left for Town . . . Caught the train to Boscombe and joined my little family at Southbourne at teatime, found them in comfortable quarters in a nice safe place and there I had a complete rest celebrating a quiet and happy Christmas. Made excursions to Bournemouth, Poole and Christchurch, the place was crowded and but for shortages and some perfunctory Lighting Restriction one would not know there was a War on.

'On my way back I stayed Sunday and Monday in Town, making many calls and on Monday afternoon assisted the Lord

Mayor and Sheriffs at an Entertainment to Children at the Guildhall and afterwards drove to the Mansion House with our old friend Sheriff Blades in his State Coach, who afterwards saw me off at the station. I wrote a full account of this to South-bourne and heard that Judith was quite satisfied that I had driven through London in Cinderella's Coach and been to see Dick Whittington.'

1918
  Cooper ends his 64-page journal: 'It is the greatest treat to have one's Sundays free again and I think the Public have very little notion of the work that has been done by the Volunteers during the last two years and still look upon them much as they did the old Volunteer Corps of 1915. My Battalion is 611 strong and Suffolk Coy boasts 5,188 trained Volunteers.'
  Volunteer activities predominate in his account of the last year of the war. The Germans' spring offensive, their last great bid to win the war, was watched in Britain with deepening concern. With the conscription age raised to 51 in April, and all available troops being rushed to the front, the role of the Volunteers became a crucial one and Cooper trained with one of the Special Service Companies that were formed with the very real possibility of having to fight on the beaches. Although he relinquished some of his other responsibilities, he saw the war out with energies unabated, his cool, wry appraisal of everything that went on around him perceptive to the last.
  '*14 Jan.* This night the Huns bombarded Yarmouth again, putting in 50 to 60 shells in seven minutes, killing seven and wounding many more ... The next night set in the sharpest frost known here since 1894–5, I had four pipes burst and 140 houses in the town suffered in the same way ...
  '*16 Jan.* Six inches of snow in the night and the next night it rained in torrents. That afternoon I went on to my marshes after some wild geese with my Musketry Instructor, we saw a

single goose and stalked it to within 100 yds, he wounded it with a service rifle and we followed the blood marks about half a mile in the snow and eventually I killed it, a white fronted goose in fine condition, so end all wild goose chases . . .

'*21 Jan*. This night I retired from the Fire Brigade after 23 years service, 11 as Lieutenant and 12 as Captain. I intended to see the War out but it is lasting too long and I do not wish for another three years of war conditions and Air raid Watches. I have been fortunate in avoiding any serious fires during my time in the town especially since so many troops have been stationed here. They did set the Centre Cliff on fire one night in bitter cold when the water froze as it dripped from the Standpipe but we quickly had it out. My theory and practice has always been to get on to a fire at the earliest possible moment and have made a start with the Handcart alone sometimes . . .

'The wildfowl season has been extended to the 31 Mch and I have for some time been shooting for Mr Pol regularly twice a week, for the week ending Sat the 23rd we have shot 10 duck, 3 snipe, a plover, a hare and 2 mogos, quite useful and I am able to send regularly to the Missis, as her meat ration at Southbourne is only 6 to 8 oz. per week and she has to stand in a queue to get it . . .

'*27 Feb*. Sitting in the office this morning I heard the Lifeboat Gun, hurried home for my bicycle and burberry and arrived at the Harbour just as the Boat shoved off, I jumped into her as she passed the next Landing Stage and the Signalman chucked my belt in after me, it happened they were a hand short so I made up the crew. They told me it was a seaplane in trouble. We had a fine run off about two miles, wind at west and could see cargo and patrol vessels coming in from sea in response to wireless calls from the Naval Base no doubt. Just before we arrived one of our fishing boats which was in the Bight at the time, got there and took the pilot off, one of the floats and part of the plane was underwater and would have sunk in time, then a Patrol Boat came along took the pilot on board and towed the plane away, we sailed home and within $1\frac{1}{2}$ hours I was back in the office.

'After this it was rather tedious work during the afternoon taking down evidence as Magistrates Clerk the whole afternoon on the prosecution of a number of Military Offenders against the Lighting Restrictions, one feels sorry for these because they are put into empty houses with no blinds and are not given anything to cover the windows with, so they have to use their Ground Sheets. Still as has been explained by the Bench on many occasions our only safety is in absolute darkness, occasionally a light shews seawards, then the Patrol Boats wireless to the Naval Base and they telephone to the Police who forthwith send out and discover the offender. Going home in Southwold on a really dark night reminds one of the blindman who hunted in a dark room for a black hat that wasn't there . . .

'*12 Mar.* The Council have taken over all the vacant building plots on the Town Farm Estate and let the greater part of it as allotments. The owners refused to let them have it last year so this year with the help of the Suffolk War Agricultural Committee we commandeered it. The Mayor took up and gardened a plot next the Girl Guides Room which was occupied by soldiers, after his crops were nicely up, they converted the building into a gas chamber for which it was quite unfitted, of course the gas escaped and the Mayor's onions were badly gassed . . .

'*20–26 March.* We have been watching most anxiously the news from the Western Front during the great German attack, we have not heard the guns this time nor has the battle brought on the usual torrents of rain at present altho' today it is snowing and very cold. The Germans seem to time their offensives better than we do as regards weather conditions, up to yesterday this has been one of the sunniest and warmest Marches I recollect but on Sunday last we began Summer time and perhaps this upset the weather, my people are returning from the south coast today which is very unlucky . . .

'*1 April*. Easter Monday. I went up to work in the garden but was soon called home, an urgent message for my adjutant to report to Headquarters at Ipswich ... From what one has heard since I feel sure the Volunteers were on the brink of mobilisation this Easter time and the position was most critical ...

'*15 April*. Up Wolseys Creek to shift the *Louie* down to put her on slip after being up there three years. Turned out a dreadful day, north gale and heavy rain, all got very wet, the next two days were torrential rains and floods all about, the Mail Van got stuck in Holton Run, this synchronises again with the heavy German Push near Ypres ...

'*29 April to 4 May*. I was busy during this period in recruiting Volunteers in the country villages, the War Agricultural Committee having sent out circulars to all workers protected by them urging them to join. I held evening meetings at Flixton, Rumburgh, St Lawrence, Wrentham, Wangford, Mutford, Barnby, Kessingland, Huntingfield and two at Lowestoft at all of which I spoke and pressed home the very critical state on the Western Front and the duty of every man to train. The response was useful but not great and the work of organising and training all these small sections was very considerable.

'I was particularly interested by the Huntingfield Meeting, as I called first at the Hall where my Gt Grandfather R. I. Cooper lived till 1819 and with another Gt Grandfather B. Woolnough helped to raise and train Volunteers during the Napoleonic Wars, both becoming officers of the Corps. I have the sword of one and a Silver Teapot presented to the other when the Corps was disbanded in 1813. I spoke from a waggon on the Village Green and the surroundings must have been almost the same a hundred years ago ...

'*4 June*. The Scheme came out for Special Service Companies of Volunteers to undertake active service on the coast and I went to Ipswich Headquarters about it, the first to give in my name. (We were not told the reason for the call but know now that England was being denuded of troops to hold up the German Offensive and replace our enormous casualties and it was necessary to take men from the East Coast and send them out to France and the Volunteers were asked to find 15,000 men to replace these until the Americans arrived in force. We understood we were to hold the coast until the troops in the depots and camps were rushed up in case of attack but we have good reason to believe that most of the available men from the camps had already gone and no doubt the position was critical in the extreme.) During the week I attended Parades all over my area to explain the Scheme . . .

'29 *June*. Left home to take command of a Special Service Company, 84 strong, at Bawdsey Manor near Felixstowe. The men went under canvas and most of the officers but Capt Barratt and I got into an empty room in the Stables. We started training at once with the 2/8 Essex, Cyclists, and took our share in the ordinary routine of the Coastal defences . . . I hired a furnished cottage from the Estate and fetched my people there on the 22 July so that we had a very comfortable and enjoyable time having the run of the Manor Grounds. I fired the G.M. Course at Colchester and came out at the head of my Company and tied for second place among all the officers. I completed my time with the Special Service Company on the 26 Aug. and altho' with many others I was willing to stay if wanted it was clear that the situation was very much easier, we were turning the tables on the Germans in France and the Americans were arriving in large numbers and the War Office was therefore no longer in urgent need of the Volunteers and I was of course glad to be able to return to my work . . .

'30 *August*. Returned to Southwold by car from Bawdsey and found the Town full of visitors, the best season since 1914, either people have more confidence in the safety of the E. Coast or they are getting tired of the S. and W. Coasts . . .

'12 *Oct*. The Hants C.O. sent for me today and stated that the Lifeboathouse windows and doors are to be sandbagged up for defence and pill boxes built, one at the Harbour, one on S. Green just opposite my house, one on Haven Beach Marshes and one at the corner of Corporation Rd, this does not look like the end of the War, altho' we have all been feeding on Peace rumours and the Collapse of Turkey and Germany, most people are very sceptical about the German proposals and no doubt the Military Authorities think a last flare up and an attempt on England will be the last German trump. (These Works were not carried out.) . . .'

By this time Britain was in the grip of a scourge more deadly than Zeppelins or Gothas—'Spanish Influenza'. This mysterious disease spread round the world and in less than a year had killed over 70 million people, many more than were killed in the entire war. By the end of October the death-roll in Britain had reached 4,000. By the time the epidemic subsided in May 1919, it had killed nearly 200,000.

There is a tragic irony to the ending of Cooper's journal, with the town that for four years had lived in dread of air raids, bombardments and invasion and which still bristled with pill-boxes, barbed wire and gun emplacements, defenceless in the last weeks of the war against a virulent germ.

'When I was at Bawdsey Camp we got the first wave of Spanish Flu and the men went down very quickly. We had 70 cases in a few days but in most instances it was mild and I escaped. With the autumn, after weeks of wet and wind from the S. and S.E. and the most unparalleled slaughter in Flanders, comes a much more serious form of Flu into the Town and by the latter part of Oct and early Novr it was raging and several deaths occurred. One woman was quite well at noon and dead next morning, whole families were in bed at once and it spread in the most wholesale manner.

'Homes and I gave a shooting party of nine guns and several ladies joined us at lunch including my wife, the doctor said he was not feeling well and left after a snack and a drink, within a couple of days nine of that party were down with Flu. One strong healthy sportsman suddenly felt ill and got up to go to bed but fell down in a faint altho' he told me he had never fainted before. My wife went down and the next day Judith developed it, I had one day in bed but escaped the real thing. My neighbour Docura of the Red Lion kept about with it too long then went to bed and was dead in no time, a fine strong man but too fat.

'Strangely enough only about 20 cases occurred amongst the troops, these were at once isolated, all indoor functions and gatherings were stopped, the men were kept out of doors and not allowed to go to pubs or shops and so the thing was checked. One result was that the proposed big Inspection of Volunteers at Norwich on the 3rd Novr. was cancelled, a very good thing as it turned out an awful day and must have been followed by serious results . . .

'*9 Nov.* We reelected Mr Pipe our Victory Mayor as we hope, and building upon the urgent request of the Germans for an Armistice and the marvellous successes of the Allied Armies everywhere, all felt quietly optimistic and the chief topic was of reconstruction after peace. At lunch afterwards the Vicar took a cigar to smoke after the Declaration saying that he had renounced smoking for the period of the War, which prompted me when speaking to relate my vow not to buy any new clothes during the War and that I was then wearing a prewar suit, at which Mr Alderman and Tailor Denny cried "Shame!" and we all laughed quite like in ante war days.

'It is strange how very quietly everyone here is taking the sudden prospect of an early peace, either owing to the sickness everywhere or to the people having steeled themselves to another and a harder winter of war and not wishing to shout until well outside the wood.

'*10 Nov.* The Mayor went to Church very quietly on account of the Flu and uncertainty of the outlook. I was not well enough to go and I hear that seven Councillors were absent and that it was the smallest muster on record.

'*11 Nov.* I went to the office and at 11 was rung up by the County Adjutant who told me that the Armistice had been signed and that guns were firing and bells ringing at Ipswich. I did not take it in at first and could hear him shouting "War is over" at the other end. I hurried down to the Mayor and found he had just received the news and in a few minutes a car came in from the Covehithe Air Station full of mad Officers, cheering, waving flags and blowing trumpets. Flags soon came out, the Bells began to ring and a few of us adjourned to the Mayor's house and cracked some bottles of Fizz. An impromptu Meeting was called and the Mayor read the official Telegram from the Swan Balcony, some soldiers came up on a waggon with the Kaiser in effigy, which they tied to the Town Pump and burnt amidst cheers.

'At 12.45 we went to a short thanksgiving service at the Church and nearly all work was knocked off for the day but the Town took it very quietly on the whole. The Band played at the Mess in the evening and there were some squibs and cheering on the Green etc. The Town Pump and a few other lamps were lit up, also the Lighthouse which I do not think has been alight half a dozen times since the War, the fun finished soon after ten.

'The only sad event was poor Docura's funeral which took place with Military Honours in the afternoon, great respect being paid by the Hants. and I think every one felt it doubly sad that a man of 37 and a keen Volunteer from the start should be buried amidst the Armistice rejoicings. As a rule he was the last man I saw on my return from Fire Duty and I think he felt it was all over safely if he saw me go home to bed.'

NOTES
ON CONTRIBUTORS

Notes on Contributors

Where certain biographical details are contained in a chapter, they are not repeated in these notes.

1 Cavalryman in the Flying Machines

William Ronald Read died at his home in Sussex in March 1972, a bachelor aged 87. His diaries came to light thanks to a routine check by the Imperial War Museum, who wrote to the executor after seeing his obituary notice in a newspaper.

The third child of seven, and the eldest son, Read was left very well provided for on the death of his father, an inventor and industrial technologist who amassed a fortune while still a comparatively young man. After retiring from the RAF in 1932 he devoted himself to travel, sporting activities and to training his string of steeplechasers and hurdlers. Rejoining in 1939 he served through the last war as Inspector of National Savings in RAF Establishments.

During the ten years from 1945 Read made a series of remarkable solo journeys by Land Rover, including Cape Town to Cairo, Cape Town to Algiers and two crossings of the Sahara. In his 70th year he drove across Europe and the Middle East to revisit the places in India he had known as a young cavalry officer.

Mr G. R. E. Brooke, one of his five nephews, writes: 'He was unquestionably daring but he also possessed an innate prudence and resourcefulness which served to secure his survival through a lifetime of varied adventure. He was self-reliant and self-willed, but quiet and modest, combining a Victorian moral outlook with an Edwardian taste for the good things in life. His acts of generosity were numerous but one never heard much about them.

'A man of action, he never sought publicity. His manuscript autobiography was written for personal amusement. He had no pretentions to being an intellectual and his literary preferences were centred on the writings of Rider Haggard, Conan Doyle and the verses of FitzGerald's *Rubáiyát of Omar Khayyám*, in which he found lasting delight.'

2 Death Wish in No Man's Land

William St Leger's Western Front diary, in the form of a bound typescript copy of 590 pages, was discovered by Peter Eaton, a second-hand bookseller in Notting Hill Gate, London, among the piles of old books, manuscripts and letters that are regularly brought in to him by dustmen, rag-and-bone merchants and barrow boys from all parts of London. 'It makes one very angry to think of material of such historic value being thrown away', he says. 'I have no means of knowing now where this volume came from. It was obviously good enough to include in my catalogue, which goes to institutions and private collectors in many parts of the world.'

The diary copy was acquired by the Imperial War Museum in April 1971. They are now hoping that an earlier diary St Leger mentions as having kept during his active service with the Cape Town Highlanders in German South-West Africa will one day also come to light.

3 Slaughter on the Somme

The Rev J. M. S. Walker's newsletters were recently typed out and sent to the Imperial War Museum by his younger son, Mr M. L. Walker, a retired chemical engineer living at Wimbledon, London. 'Some of the originals, hastily scribbled in pencil as well as ink, would be indecipherable to those not used to his handwriting', he says.

Mr Walker, whose elder brother, a former public school master, died in 1969, can clearly recall the Christmas holidays of 1916 when his father returned from the Somme to the Lincolnshire rectory, with its orchards and spacious flower-beds, croquet-lawn and tennis court. 'To me he seemed in no way changed by his experiences. He was a level-headed, cheerful man, who enjoyed an occasional practical joke—there was at times something of the small boy in him.'

Up to his retirement in 1946 at the age of 75, Walker was happy in the quiet but busy life of a parish priest, from 1919 to 1928 as Rector of Great Billing, Northants, from 1928 to 1946 as Rector of Steeple Aston, Oxfordshire, both college livings. He retired to Fleet, Hants, where he died in 1955, his wife dying a year later. His obituary in the local paper noted him particularly as a pillar of the Fleet Horticultural Society.

4 *Tommy Atkins, PBI*

Ernest Atkins sent a copy of his journal to the BBC and in his long letter seems almost desperately anxious to get over the viewpoint of the ordinary Tommy for the forthcoming television series. Under the heading 'Descriptions of Battles' he indicates the bewilderment that was as much a part of the PBI's lot as danger and privation.

'Ordinary soldiers could not describe battles. We did not know one was taking place often (shades of Monty explaining to his men the battle plans). We were told that we were not there to think, only to obey. We marched here, we marched there, we heard the thunder of the guns, we went into action, we came out and went in somewhere else. Sometimes hurried from one point to another and when it was over we were told that was the second battle of Ypres or Messines or what have you. Our people at home sometimes told us in letters.'

5 *A Lad Goes to War*

Bert Chaney was born in Hackney in 1896. 'My father was a compositor and, as was the done thing in those days, apprenticed me to the same trade,' he writes. 'He was a bit of a show-off and was very fond of going to war, first as a signaller to South Africa in 1900, and then as a member of the RAMC. In 1911 he went to Turkey during some sort of war that was going on out there and was very proud of the medal he received from Queen Alexandra herself. He thought she was God.

'Naturally he had to join up for World War I. This somewhat changed his feelings for the glories of war, though afterwards, still proud of his army service, he showed off his string of medals whenever possible. I, on the other hand, had no illusions about a land fit for heroes—anyhow, all the real heroes were dead—and on more than one occasion nearly threw my three medals away.'

In 1934 Chaney obtained a job as Works Manager to a Dublin firm of printers, where he remained until his retirement in 1964. He lives with his wife at Mount Merrion, County Dublin. 'We had no children, and used to spend our spare time doing a double act, magic, mental telepathy and puppetry. My health having forced me to take things more easily, I now fill in time during the winter evenings writing, with the typewriter on my knees in front of the fire—memories of my childhood, the war book, now a blood-and-thunder detective story. But don't run away with the idea that I am a doddering old man. I still keep the lawn front and back of the house in order, and do quite a lot of the interior decorating.'

6 All for a Shilling a Day

William Pressey, born in Birmingham in 1895, with four elder sisters, attended a church school until he was 14. Though 'a bit of a tearaway—the police getting at me for playing football in the streets, letting off fireworks etc.'—he developed a gift for sketching and painting and attended art school during four years in a small engineering firm before enlisting.

When he joined the General Electric Company at Witton in 1931 it was the tenth job he had taken since demobilisation, but it lasted thirty years until his retirement in 1961. His wife died four years later, when he sold everything and went to live in a cousin's farmhouse near Romsey, Hants. There he lives contentedly, with a private sitting-room overlooking the farmyard, a bedroom facing cornfields, woods and the river Blackwater, where he fishes in between doing jobs around the farm. Three times a week he motors to Romsey in his MG car to do the shopping. 'I am also a good do-it-yourself man', he writes, 'and have all sorts of tools, some used by my father, bless him, 50 or more years ago.'

7 Gallipoli—the Great Beyond

Norman King-Wilson, a lieutenant-colonel (retd), died at his home at Parry Sound, Ontario, in May 1972 in his 88th year. Born in Richmond Hill, Ontario, he studied medicine at Toronto University and took an advanced course at Edinburgh University. He served as ship's surgeon with P and O Shipping Lines, travelling extensively in the Mediterranean and South America, before setting up in private practice with his father in Toronto in 1913. He was married on the day war was declared.

After being invalided back to England from Gallipoli, he joined the Canadian Army and served until after the Armistice when he returned to Toronto to become head of the Ear, Nose and Throat Department of the Western Hospital. Active in the Canadian Territorial Army since 1903, he commanded the Governor-General's Horse Guards from 1929 to 1933. During the last war he held staff appointments with the Canadian Army Medical Corps. He remained active after retirement, opening a marina and post office near his home, taking courses in advanced navigation with the Power Squadron. His wife died in 1963.

A copy of King-Wilson's Gallipoli journal was found among the papers of the late Frank Brownson, his brother-in-law, in England, and sent to the Imperial War Museum. From his home in Willowdale, Ontario, his only son, Patrick King-Wilson, who has six children and one grandchild, writes: 'I am sure my father would have been very pleased to know that his journal was being used in this book. It is too bad that he is not alive to see it.'

8 Battle of Jutland Survivor

Petty Officer Ernest Francis' letter is one of a number of eye-witness accounts of episodes during the battle of Jutland from which historians have taken extracts to build up a composite picture of the engagement. It gains considerably in dramatic effect by being used here in its entirety.

9 Front Line, Home Front

Ernest Read Cooper's original diary is in the possession of his daughter, Miss Judith E. Cooper, who lives at Woodbridge, Suffolk, to which the family moved from Southwold in 1931, some eleven years after Cooper had retired from his position as Town Clerk and his practice as a solicitor. He had deposited a copy with the Imperial War Museum some time before his death in 1948 at the age of 83.

Miss Cooper writes: 'Though my father retired as a comparatively young man he was never dull for a moment during his latter years. He published three books on Suffolk, *A Suffolk Coast Garland*, *Mardles from Suffolk* and a lifeboat book, *Storm Warriors of the Suffolk Coast*. He wrote frequent articles for the local press and for seafaring journals, and contributed a number of papers to the Suffolk Institute of Archaeology. He maintained his keen interest in the home-based Militia, and an address he delivered to the Militia Club in 1926, in which he traced the history of the Militia from earliest times until the present, was published in pamphlet form.

'He was a prodigious keeper of journals and, as well as the War Diary, I have three or four yachting logs, several books of "Southwoldiana" as he called it, family histories and complete family trees. I should think no letter or note received throughout a long life was ever thrown away, and since my mother's death in 1967 it has taken me about six months to go through them all. As I am no better at throwing things away than he was, his papers are mostly stored in boxes in my cupboards, and as his period recedes in history I hope they may be of some social interest in the future. I find them very entertaining to read, and enlivened by the natural comments he used to include.'

ACKNOWLEDGEMENTS

Acknowledgements

I am greatly indebted to the Imperial War Museum for access to recently acquired war diaries and journals. I would like particularly to thank Mr Roderick Suddaby, Head of the Department of Documents, for his expert assistance in selecting material, and to Dr Christopher Dowling, Keeper of the Department of Education and Publications, for general advice.

People at War would not have been possible to compile without the support and encouragement of the Editor of *The Sunday Times*, Mr Harold Evans, and thanks are also due to Mr Michael Randall, Senior Managing Editor, Mr Derrik Mercer, News Editor, and Mr George Darby, Editorial Manager.

Finally I would like to thank all those readers of *The Sunday Times* who submitted journals, diaries, letters and personal anecdotes in answer to our request for war stories. Space could only be found for a very small proportion, but all the material submitted has been passed on to the Imperial War Museum.

M.M.